The ABLE QUEEN

Memoirs of an Indiana Hump Pilot Lost in the Himalayas

ROBERT BINZER,
as told to RAINY HORVATH

Perfect Storm Press
Scarsdale, NY

The Able Queen

ISBN: 9781736163405 (Paperback)
ISBN: 9781736163412 (Ebook)

LCCN: 2020923058

Published by: Perfect Storm Press
Cover Designer: Michelle Fairbanks

CONTENTS

Dedicated to every brave pilot
who flew off into the unknown
in defense of our nation

1st Lt. Robert Dean Binzer, 27th Troop Carrier Squadron,
US Army Air Corps – 14th Airforce

MILITARY FLIGHT TIMES
& DECORATIONS

FLYING TIME
27TH TRANSPORT SQUADRON

- Total Combat Hours: 623:45
- Total Combat Missions: 317
- Total Instrument Time: 52:50
- Total Night Flight Time: 17:30

SERVICE MEDALS AWARDED

- Air Medal
  w/ Two Oak Leaf Clusters
- Distinguished Flying Cross
  w/ One Oak Leaf Cluster
- Asiatic-Pacific Theater Ribbon
  w/ One Bronze Star
- American Defense Ribbon
- China War Memorial Medal

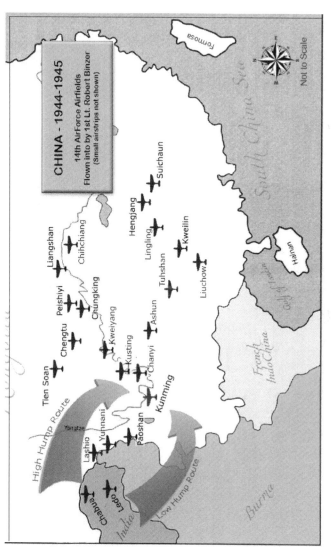

Airfields and Air Strips regularly flown into by the 14th Airforce

FOREWORD

They called it "The Aluminum Trail." There were so many crashed planes along the route between India and China that they almost created a trail that could be followed from the air.

Flying "The Hump," the route over the Himalayas between India and China, was some of the most dangerous flying in the world. Thirty-thousand-foot peaks, unpredictable winds, and Japanese fighters were just some of the perils that awaited flyers. Yet, they persevered.

The pilots were young and well-trained, but not for what awaited them in the skies over the Hump. Most of them had signed up to defend their country and for the adventure of piloting their own plane to do so.

Robert Dean Binzer was one of these young men, and what follows is his story of adventure in the service of his country. He, too, would face the perils of the Himalayas and the deadly call of the Aluminum Trail.

Follow him in his own words from training, across the ocean to India, rescuing downed pilots, and finally stepping out the door of the failing "Able Queen" to become one of those needing rescue.

This is a story that needs to be told, a unique story of the greatest generation. It could be the story of hundreds of young Americans who sought the adventure of flying and found it while serving their country in the far-off China-Burma-India Theater of World War II.

Carl W. Weidenburner, November 2020

PREFACE

This memoir is a first-person account of my father's experiences in China as a CBI Hump Pilot during World War II. Memoir is a subgenre of autobiography and differs in that it presents the authors' reflections and personal feelings about the events going on around them. Robert Binzer never stopped telling his story, sharing what happened and how he felt about it with those who would listen, and I am here now to share his stories with you.

Dad's last words were, "Sometimes an old man just needs a little help," and I promised him that I would publish this memoir for him. My work on this manuscript began that day. My role has been to collect, collate, sequence, and combine his separate writings into one comprehensive tale of one young American pilot's adventures and narrow escapes as an aviator during World War II.

To complete his story, I researched facts, verified locations and dates, added transitional text and expository details where needed, added footnotes to clarify discrepancies, selected photographs, wrote the Preface and Epilogue

Reflection, designed the original cover, and created a high-resolution map.

Writing in the vernacular and context of the day, which was the mindset and mental context of a people engaged in a bloody war, the term "Jap" was used to refer to the Japanese enemy. To update this manuscript in the context of today, I have changed each such instance to "Japanese enemy," in no way intending to rewrite history or erase elements of authenticity, but rather to be sensitive to our modern times and conventions.

Although my father wrote well, he was no English teacher. To preserve his voice, and for the authenticity of this document, I did not attempt to reshape his words into perfect English grammar but left them largely as he wrote them—the words of a teenager of the 1940s. Any necessary changes were kept to a minimum.

This work in no way presents itself as an academic research paper or a military treatise. I am not a historian or a military expert, nor do I try to present myself as one; I am simply the eldest daughter of a Hump Pilot here to bring you this thrilling story of a boy from Indiana who always dreamed of flying and one day got his wish.

This book would never have come to be if it were not for the loving encouragement, tireless support and unending knowledge of my husband, John Horvath. For that, I am deeply grateful.

I am also grateful to Mindy Stockfield, adjunct professor at Sarah Lawrence College Writing Institute, for her help and support. I would be remiss in not thanking Carl Weidenburner, CBI Theater of War historian, and Dr. David Fletcher for their encouragement, contributions, historical edits, and lively discussions in unraveling the mysteries of wartime China 1944-45.

Dad's hope was to leave something for his children and grandchildren so they would not forget him, but when I began to read his story and realized what he and his fellow crew members experienced, flying primitive aircraft in a hostile land with very little support, I knew that his story would interest more than just our own little family. So, sit back, fasten your seatbelt, and prepare for a wild ride.

CHAPTER 1

CHILDHOOD FLIGHTS OF FANCY

I was one of the lucky ones—I got out. Now, I was the only one left to jump, only there was no one there to give me a little push. It was not needed, of course. I jumped clear and was falling, tumbling through the pitch-black night. I realized that I now had to pull the ripcord and get on with this business of surviving, and as I bailed out of the Able Queen that cold night in February and watched her disappear behind the clouds, I looked up at the stars and wondered how I got here...

I was born in tiny Waynetown, Indiana, July 28, 1922—at home, which was not uncommon in those days because there was no hospital in town back then and money was scarce.

In 1926, my family moved, first to Crawfordsville, Indiana, and then on to Hammond, Indiana, for better job prospects. Jobs were hard to come by then, and better prospects in bigger towns meant my parents, Elsie and Harry "Doc" Binzer, would move again several times to follow work.

My mother, Elsie Conner Binzer, found a job there selling cosmetics in Frank's Department Store. At Christmas time, the department store had a Santa Claus that brought a pony with him. Our family picture album still has the picture of me on that pony, along with my mom and Santa Claus. People see that and think we were rich, but believe me, we were not.

I guess things were pretty rough in Hammond in spite of the jobs, as the racketeers blew up the State Theater because they would not pay them for protection. We lived very near there, and I got a good razzing as the loud explosion never woke me up.

Soon after, I was looking out the front window one night, watching traffic, when a car stopped across the street in front of the A&P store that had closed for the night. Two men got out of a big touring car and proceded to throw a brick of some kind through the front door of the store. My folks heard the noise and came running in, asking, "What happened?"

When I told them, they called the police. I guess the police came fast enough that they caught the men pilfering the store and we got a nice fruit basket and other things from the store to thank us for calling the police. But this was just too scary for my parents, so my family moved on to Gary this time, a few miles east of Hammond.

In 1933, we moved again, this time to Chicago. Now, we rented an apartment building on the corner of 79th and Laughlin Street, the South Side of Chicago. It didn't seem much different from living in Gary, except we had more streetcars. These streetcars had the entrance at the rear end and the exit at the front, and the price was seven cents with a transfer. You could get almost anywhere on the streetcars, and a Sunday pass would allow you to ride all day long if you wished.

There was an empty lot next to our apartment building that served as a place to run for the neighbor kids, and there were lots of kids around, as I recall. We kids all had great fun playing outside and climbing trees in the area. Our side of the street had hardly any trees to climb, but on the other side of the street were some great trees.

I loved to climb up the biggest tree as high as I could so I could see the airplanes out at Midway Airport. There were air races going on out there, and I would occasionally see some racing in the distance.

An Italian military aviator[1] led a squadron of seaplanes, twenty-four, if I recall correctly, flying into Chicago once. Back then, in the early days of flight, it was as thrilling to us as seeing a spaceship landing might be to people today.

---

[1] Italo Balbo's Crociera del Decennale featured the so-called "Italian Air Armada" from 1 July to 12 August, 1933. Twenty-four seaplanes flew round-trip from Rome to the Century of Progress in Chicago, Illinois, as part of an eight-leg journey. Chicago renamed the former 7th Street "Balbo Drive" and staged a parade in his honor. They flew from Chicago to New York City escorted by 36 US airplanes. Balbo was featured on the 26 June 1933 cover of *Time*. Chicago Tribune, May 6, 1997.

The Italian military planes landed in Lake Michigan over near the Navy Pier, and we made it a point to go over there and see them floating in the water just off the pier. Later, as they flew back East, I watched them go from my treetop and I dreamed of going with them.

Another great thing for me were the dirigibles that flew to Chicago. These were great times for a kid that loved airplanes. I saw the US Akron fly, along with a German ship, I think was the Hindenburg.[2] Aviation was still new to a lot of people, and I believe everyone was fascinated by the thought of flying through the air.

When the Chicago World's Fair started in 1933, we rode the streetcar down to Vincennes Street, and then transferred to the downtown route that would take us out to the Fair Grounds that was right by the Aquarium and Soldiers Field. I had been to the fair several times and was finally allowed to take visitors there on my own.

Later, after the fair was over in 1934, this whole island became Meigs Field. In 2003, the mayor of Chicago bulldozed the runways at night, which, of course, closed the field permanently. It is still closed to this day, and there are still many lawsuits pending over this act by the then-mayor.

The big thing after school was *radio*. Radio was something new, and not everyone had a radio to listen to. In the evenings, there were several stations on the air that aired

---

[2] The German Graf Zeppelin flew above Chicago in 1929, and again in 1933, over the World's Fair of 1933. Chicago Tribune, May 6, 1997; WBEZ Radio Archives.

mystery programs and comedy programs, and every station had a kids' program for after school. They were very popular, and I remember in particular that cereal box top deals were a big thing.[3]

I saved up our Wheaties box tops and sent them off and got back a small book on learning to fly. I read it from cover to cover. It must have been pretty well-written and made good sense, for years later, when I really did learn to fly in the Army, I recalled every single move in that little book.

One day in flight school, our instructor asked me if I had ever taken flying lessons before. I answered that I had "read up some on the subject," and let it go at that. I never did tell him that I really learned how to fly from a cereal box top offer booklet from Wheaties.

Eventually, my parents moved us to Valparaiso, Indiana. The street we lived on was very rough because the Interurban had tracks running down the center of the street and the bricks had settled in between the ties, making that part of the street pretty rough traveling. We jokingly called it Washboard Avenue, but the house was large, and I had my own room for the first time ever.

After my twelfth birthday, I got a job offer from the man who ran the shoe repair shop on the corner, a

---

[3] In 1931, Quaker Oats sponsored the "Man's Wings, How to Fly" box-top premium booklet, and in 1937, Post Bran Flakes sponsored the "Captain Hawk's Sky Patrol Flight Manual" premium giveaway. In 1945, Wheaties sponsored the "How to Fly" box-top premium booklet. It is likely that Bob Binzer read all of these, and certain that he read at least one.

half-block up towards town. He needed me to sweep and clean the shop. His name was Kouloff—*Mr.* Kouloff to me.

Mr. Kouloff lived in an apartment at the rear of the store, and in the evenings, if you were near, you could see and hear him playing his violin in the shop. I guess he was quite a musician. He was very good to me and paid me a quarter for my work.

He was very proud of having come here from Russia and becoming an American citizen, and he always had an American flag flying in front of his shop. After the war was over and I had a chance to visit Valparaiso, I made it a point to stop and see Mr. Kouloff with my uniform on. He was real happy and thankful that I remembered him, and I was proud to show him my medals. A little kindness goes a long way.

The 'Blitz Boys'

Man's Wings, How to Fly, 1931, Quaker Oats Premium
and Captain Frank Hawk's Sky Patrol Pilot's Manual, 1937,
Post Bran Flakes Premium were likely read by young Bob Binzer.

CHAPTER 2

I ENLIST

I am jumping ahead now, so to speak. Why did I enlist when I did? Europe was coming apart, Germany was invading and capturing countries left and right, and Russia was afraid there would be nothing left for them, so they took Finland, Estonia, and more. It seemed pretty obvious to everyone that, before long, we would become involved in this struggle.

In 1940, the draft began, and all men in the United States aged 21-40 had to register for the draft. This was something new to all of us! I was 17 years old then, but these ages dropped quickly to "all men aged 18-45." Everyone was amazed to hear that within 12 months, they expected to have 900,000 draftees on the lines.

Today, many people forget that by the end of World War II, 16 million Americans fought in the war. Of those, 50 million had registered for the draft and 10 million of them had been inducted into service. Nobody could have imagined such a thing as this, before then.

Everyone was defense-minded, and since I was no different, I purchased an MI Garand rifle from the civilian marksmanship program. This type of rifle was widely used in World War II, but I did not have a rifle of this type then, and I wanted to be ready.

The MI Garand was perhaps the finest weapon in our arsenal. World War II was won because of our having this weapon, along with some other great equipment, and I am proud to have one for my very own. When I enlisted in April of 1941, this rifle was issued only to the Infantry or other branches of the service, but still having this authentic rifle as an item from the war brings back a lot of memories of my early days as a recruit, even though this was not the same rifle that I was issued by the Army.

Between Christmas and New Year's of 1941, my family moved to Richmond, Virginia, over the holidays. By then, we all knew that we would get involved in the War in Europe sooner rather than later, and as I had turned 18, I enlisted in the Army Air Corps in April of 1941.

As a recruit entering the Air Corps at McDill Field in Tampa, Florida, in April of 1941, I had many doubts and fears concerning our ability to fight a war against the Nazis, let alone win it. As for myself, I did not want to wait until the draft called on me, for if that happened, I knew it was very doubtful that I would get a choice in which branch of the service I might be placed, so I went down and enlisted.

I had always wanted to fly and decided on the newly formed Army Air Corps, but worried that I would not pass the eye test to be a pilot due to some vision problems. Fortunately for me, my dad, "Doc" Binzer, was an ophthalmologist. He shared my concern and helped me memorize the eye chart, and I passed the test with flying colors.

McDill Field

All the men in my barracks had enlisted to be in the Army Air Corps, and we all felt like we knew for sure that we, the people of the United States, would be in this war sooner rather than later, so we had better be ready. In my early training at McDill Field, we only had World War I equipment for training.

The first rifles we were trained with for close order drill were the 1903 Springfield 30.06. We also trained with the .45 caliber automatic pistol, also designed for and used in World War I. Now, we were issued our first real uniforms, which were really World War I uniforms, along with the World War I steel helmets, and for daily use, we were issued two fatigue suits, which were like coveralls buttoned up the front.

Leftover World War I uniforms were all they had available at this point in time, and the uniform that I was issued even had holes in the jacket! They were probably moth holes, but an 18-year-old kid might imagine the holes as being bullet holes. Today, I realize that of course these were not bullet holes at all, but moth holes from being in storage for perhaps 23 years or so.

We had no idea what the other branches of the Army or Navy were facing as far as equipment, and we knew they were trying to quickly build an Army, but we were wondered how we were ever going to win a war like this with old equipment. However, by the time our first 30 days were up, we all had new uniforms, and our confidence in the Army Air Corps was revived.

McDill was not a basic training center for recruits, as the Infantry had at various locations; this was an operational airbase that had transitional training for Bomb Squadrons. The aircraft we were to be trained on was the B17 Bomber. The base also had a bombing range off somewhere in the area.

Recruits like myself were used to fill up the table of organization for various squadrons located at McDill, and the particular squadron I found myself in was an air base squadron. We learned that we would not be in charge of McDill Air Force Base, not ever. Our training would be for running an air base somewhere else at some time in the future. As recruits, we received training in our assigned areas.

Our first training was some close order drilling—this is the way you learned to stand in formation and march together in an orderly manner. At first, this was done without weapons, for with our new GI shoes and not being familiar with commands we had a lot to learn, and weapons were still too much.

Our first drill sergeant was not a sergeant at all; he was a private, just like the rest of us. However, he had been in the Marine Corps, and after his enlistment was up in the Marines, he was a civilian for a while, until the war effort came along. He was older than most of us, and it was obvious that he was in charge of teaching us something about becoming soldiers.

He was firm and fair, and it did not take too long to realize this was our drill sergeant, and we had better pay attention to what he said. After a while, we were given some written tests to see what jobs we could qualify for. At the time of enlistment, you were asked what sort of job you would be interested in, and I had chosen aerial photographer.

When the test scores came back, I found that I had qualified for aerial photographer training, but the school for this was in Denver, Colorado, and there was a long backlog of people ahead of me who had already been accepted.

My test scores also qualified me for several other jobs, but it was recommended to me by the squadron commander that I go to the Teletype maintenance course at Chanute Field, Illinois, at this time, and that later on, it might be possible for me to take the course in aerial photography.

It appeared to me that I had better take the Teletype course to stay in good graces with the squadron commander, and besides, being a Teletype mechanic did not sound like too bad of a job to me at the time, with war looming on the horizon.

Chanute Field

In 1941, Army personnel traveled by railroad when just a few men were to be sent to another station. It wasn't very long before I was on a train and headed for Chanute Field, Illinois, with two others from my base. Chanute was a very large base, and it was just a school, though it may have had a runway for teaching aircraft mechanics and various other courses. They also had Teletype maintenance training, which is what I had been sent there to learn.

Chanute turned out to be an awesome experience for me. Here we were, literally thousands of us, in what was kind of like a college, but we were so busy with our own particular courses of study that we never got to see all the other schools or courses that were going on at McDill at the same time.

We were in class most of the day and also three nights during the week, but we had weekends off. Most of us went over to Champaign, Illinois, where there were big USO dances. This seemed great, as we had not been at McDill long enough to gain any privileges. These dances were a welcome addition to my training.

Early in the morning, you fell out for roll call and marched off to the mess hall for breakfast while it was still too dark out to see. Once there, you found yourself a place in line, a long line that led into a dining hall that must have fed a thousand or more at one time, cafeteria-style of course. Lunch and dinner were the same way.

We soon became acquainted with a Teletype machine and were informed that before we left this place, we would be taking these machines apart and putting them back together, blindfolded. This seemed a little far-fetched to me as there must have been over a million parts in this machine. But somehow I managed to pass the course and ended up rather liking the idea of taking care of Teletype machines.

Once we had completed the course, we were to be returned to our squadron, where I would be doing my new job. Things were a little different for us now as our squadron had moved from McDill Air Base to an air base in New Orleans, Louisiana. We were allowed a short furlough to go home and then left from home to report to the New Orleans Air Base.

I arrived at the New Orleans Air Base in the summer of 1941, though I do not recall the exact date. There were two of us there who had been to Teletype school—me and Ed Snell. We talked it over, and Snell seemed to be agreeable to take the 08:00-20:00 shift.

I was happy to take the 20:00-08:00 shift as I could then spend my leisure time during the daylight hours doing things we normally could not do. I liked this because we were not normally free to do as we wished during daylight working hours. This schedule seemed to suit us both, and things settled down to a steady pace, at least for a while.

Robert Dean Binzer 1941

CHAPTER 3

PEARL HARBOR

Pearl Harbor was a rude awakening for everyone. As I write this on December 7th, 2006, if someone asked where I was on this day in 1941 and what my first thoughts were, here is what I would tell them—I was asleep.

It was Sunday, and quiet on the New Orleans Army Air Base when Pearl Harbor was attacked. On Sundays, we had no formal formation or roll call, and for many, no duties, so it was nice to be able to sleep late and lounge around on a Sunday morning.

Not this Sunday, however, as out of nowhere a tremendous herd of sergeants blew through the barracks, awakening everyone who was still sleeping. I was told in no uncertain terms to get up, get dressed, and get the Teletype machine working as soon as fast I could. Then, I was told that the Japanese Navy had attacked Pearl Harbor. We were at war!

I nodded my understanding and grabbed my fatigues as I wondered where Pearl Harbor was. We all tried to make sense of it as we jumped into our clothes and wondered how serious this might be. I was certainly not expecting war to come at this point in my military career!

I had been trained in Teletype maintenance and was now put in charge of the Teletype Section of Air Corps Supply, New Orleans Army Air Base. We only had one Teletype machine at my station in Air Corps Supply, and I managed to get that machine going as soon as I ran into the warehouse where we kept it.

Normally, this machine was on 08:00-16:30, five days a week. But now, I was told, this machine would be on and working 24 hours a day, every day, seven days a week. No downtime was acceptable.

We kept a folding Army cot and some blankets at our station, so I was able to pull the cot up to the machine and sleep whenever there were no messages to send. Incoming messages came in automatically, and all I had to do was acknowledge that they had been received. A bell rang to alert me that it was time to acknowledge receipt of the message.

It worked out well for me. Twelve-hour days like this were no problem at all, and by 08:00, I had enough sleep and was ready for other things.

We were concerned about the whole situation, of course, but nobody really knew what would happen next. Remember, there was no news media like we have today. Also, we were well aware that we had only two aircraft on our airbase that were air-worthy—a B-18 Bomber and an 0-47 used for observation flights.

Both aircraft were obsolete as far as combat was concerned, so any defensive operation to protect our base or the city of New Orleans seemed out of the question to us. There were some Naval training bases close to us, but I had never seen anything other than training aircraft at their bases. Another Naval station on the Mississippi River was the only other military base around our area. I had never been to that river station, so I had no idea what help they might give if we were attacked.

Everyone was worried. Come daylight, the B-18 went out on patrol over the Gulf, and by-and-by, the 0-47 made a flight, which we assumed was also on Gulf patrol. We did not get a whole lot of news about Pearl Harbor, but the local newspaper had monstrous headlines. I'm not sure if there were any pictures.

As I said, we had no news media as we know it today. But we did know, from the radio reports, that there was little left of our fleet that had been in the harbor that day, and we also knew that there had been many casualties as a result of this raid by the Japanese Navy.

When Pearl Harbor happened, we were far too busy to change jobs. But as the war progressed, the powers-that-be became aware that we did not have enough pilots to be involved in the war going on in Europe. So, they called for more.

Eventually, I was accepted into Flight Training and became a pilot in the Army Air Force. I finally graduated in Advanced Flying and Tennessee Maneuvers at Brooks Field, San Antonio, Texas, in June 1943.

These were happy times for me. Training and the thrill of flying left little time to be homesick. Additional training was at an air base located at Aiken, South Carolina. It was no secret now that we were boning up for overseas. We spent nights wondering where we would be sent, talking about the possibilities, and wondering how rough it might be. As we pondered our fates, we asked ourselves the same age-old questions as any soldier/pilot while we prepared to depart.

A troop train landed us in California, and a few days later, we were loaded onto a large Pacific Ocean luxury liner turned Troopship, called the Mariposa.

The Mariposa was a beautiful ship with wood-paneled walls and a two-story-high dining room with crystal chandeliers. But that was mostly for the Brass. Still, it was a beautiful ship, and if one could forget about the guns and gun crews that were on duty day and night, one might get the feeling that this was just a nice vacation cruise.

War was closer now, and by this time, we knew what our destination would be—*China*. We learned that we would eventually fly over the "Hump," a 535-mile "sky highway" over the Himalayan mountains to our air bases somewhere "over there."

We had not expected China, and once again, we looked out at the ocean and asked ourselves the age-old questions, but not for long, because the Mariposa was the fastest transport ship in the fleet. Our next port-of-call: Bombay, India.

(L-R) Vaughn and Rollin Binzer
The "Blitz Boys"

CHAPTER 4

WHEELS UP OVER
THE HIMALAYAS

I was one of the pilots on our way to join our squadron, the 19th Liaison Squadron in Kunming, China. When I found out where I was going, I was eager to get to China. From early adolescence, I had wanted to visit China, and I usually had a good outlook toward the people there. My only concerns at the time were my hope that there would be no problems getting to know everyone at our new base, and that this trip to Kunming would bring no problems. But I made it fine, no sweat.

What was it like, you ask? Briefly, fantastic! Exciting! Certainly enlightening, and of course, there were extremely frightening times as it was very dangerous. Beautiful too—the countryside there has so many spectacular areas of beauty. These were not the places that were tourist destinations, but remote places of great beauty.

"Flying the Hump," as it was referred to, was not to be taken lightly. Flying over the most mountainous stretch of ground between India and China was a dangerous trip. There were places that had peaks that went up almost 30-thousand feet, and the temperature at that altitude was often well below -15 or more below zero (F). Flying this route, oxygen was very thin, and oxygen masks were required.

Why did we go this way? We were avoiding the Japanese enemy fighters that were also out there and trying to shoot us down, that's why. By the end of the war, there were 1,400 airmen dead, and almost 400 missing. Some were captured by the Japanese, and many were never found and never heard from again.

Kunming was an important airbase because it was located at the end of the Burma Road, which was previously cut off by the Japanese and was the end supply depot for everything coming over the Himalayan mountains by truck or ox cart. The Kunming base had been an earlier AVG strip for P-40s and the headquarters for the Governor of Yunnan Province's private troops. Now, it served as the headquarters for the 19th Liaison Squadron.

I arrived at my first base in this outfit, a small airfield northeast of Kunming that had a dirt strip airfield. It was called Yanglin, and here we were a constant target for Japanese bombers. The barracks had been built by hand by the local peasants using bricks made with clay and straw.

Our barracks had red tile roofs and charcoal-burning heaters, and we did have doors, as opposed to most houses in China, which did not have doors back then as we know them.

There was no Army PX or commissary in most of these tiniest of airfields, and we got rations once a month—a package of cigarettes, toothpaste, shaving cream, and a few essentials. We ate C-Rations or K-Rations shipped over to us, but local peasant women would wash and iron our uniforms by hand in exchange for bars of soap or a pack of cigarettes and we could hire kids to polish our boots for pennies. The Chinese natives there were always eager to help the Americans.

There were many dangers we faced in flying the Hump—to get over the Himalayan mountains, of course. The weather was unpredictable, as the Himalayan mountains create their own weather systems, not to mention the lack of communications to start with, and, of course, the Japanese enemy.

But there were other problems as well—disease and dysentery, and the fact that not all the natives were friendly. The LoLos[4] were headhunters who roamed the mountains

---

[4] Southern Sichuan was home to the Yi, also called LoLos, during WWII. Their fierce resistance to the Chinese earned them the name, "The Independent Lo-Lo of Ta-Liang Shaun." Their reputation as headhunters helped to keep British officials out of the area during their rule of Burma, and it was only slowly that Chinese Communist cadres were able to penetrate their territory in Southwest Yunnan. The mountainous Lo-Lo homelands are designated an Independent Prefecture by China to this day (*The Consolidation of the South China Frontier, George Moseley*).

near the Hump. Between them and the Japanese enemy fighters, we had our hands full.

One of the best pilots I ever knew, Robert Zalusky, was the only person who ever made friends with the LoLo headhunters. Bob was a fantastic pilot, who flew L-5s into their area, and somehow persuaded the LoLos to allow our Graves details to go into the jungle areas where they had located downed aircraft so that the bodies of our pilots could be removed from there and brought home. He could write a book about this affair, and I'm surprised he hasn't!

Binzer (*me*), being so popular with the CO, or perhaps recognized as a real leader, was soon dispatched again— this time to the frontlines base at Paoshan (Baoshan) in the far western Yunnan province, near the Burma border. I was the only officer there, with eight or nine pilots, some mechanics, one cook, and a couple of NCOs, for about three months. So, I guess I was the CO, only no one called me CO.

Paoshan was a particularly dangerous area because it was headquarters for Chiang Kai-shek's private forces. So, it was always a target for Japanese bombers, even though it was just a grass airfield in a valley between two steep mountains, with the Salween River running just a couple of blocks away from the center of town.

There were eight enlisted pilots in this squadron, and we flew Stinson L-5 Sentinels, which were small and maneuverable enough to land in tight jungle airstrips but large enough to carry roughly 3.3 tons of equipment and supplies and evacuate wounded patients. We were also an observation and reconnaissance squad, so that was another reason for the Japanese to go after us. We had other ships too, but mostly we flew the L-5s.

We were given missions to deliver bombs and gasoline to one of two airfields that were surrounded by the Japanese, and we could only get in there with fighter escort. These missions were to be during daylight hours. Once, we had to fly in such close formation that we waved to each other.

The fighters would go ahead of us, supposedly clearing the way, and it worked. We got to the surrounded airfields and made our delivery without being fired upon, but because of the constant danger of Japanese bombers, it was decided that future missions to those airfields would be at night, and with no lights or radios. We had already several missions like this, and they worked.

However, there were other problems with flying at night, among them the Japanese air raids. Our fighters were able to provide air cover to us during daytime operations, but not at night. So, when we flew night missions, we were out there on our own. This tends to sharpen the flying skills.

1st Lt. Robert Binzer, Hump Pilot

CHAPTER 5

HARD LANDING

We flew into even smaller strips than at Paoshan, if you can believe that! To the west, the northwest and the southwest, we would either haul a person, parts of a 5-inch gun, ammo, supplies, and whatever was needed in support of our advisors to the Chinese Army, which was out there searching for, or hiding from, their honorable enemy.

As flight leader, one of my jobs was to see that all our auxiliary fields were as safe as you could make them, as some of the loads we carried were not really very safe to begin with. There were 75mm artillery shells, 3-inch guns, gasoline, hand grenades, and sometimes a person needed to ride in the back seat of an L-5.

We had been in perhaps seven or eight tiny jungle strips, and it was on one of these occasions that I felt it my duty to check out a newly developed airstrip before letting my pilots go in that I crashed while taking out a wounded captain.

When we learn to fly, one maneuver that we are taught is short field takeoff. It is sometimes an interesting maneuver and depending on your location and the urgency of the need to get off the ground, sometimes this takeoff can spoil your whole day.

Our instructors always stressed the importance of having plenty of room for maneuvering, and this always made sense to me, too. In China, you did not need to be a rocket scientist for this maneuver, just a lot of common sense would do, providing things were going along at a reasonable pace.

My assignment on that day was to pick up Captain Booth, who was paralyzed with rheumatic fever and very sick. He needed a doctor, and that day, I was the one who that got the assignment. I was to pick him up at a Y-Forces building near Tien Shan. Our maps of places like this were not the best, but I already knew the way to Paoshan, where the Y-Forces doctor was to meet him, so getting there did not seem to be a problem to me.

Usually, something like this pickup was no problem, however, this was an airstrip, not yet a field, as it had not yet been checked out for a short field takeoff at that altitude, which was necessary to avoid flying into the side of a mountain. We had done this in other situations and found that there had to be some changes made, like removing short trees or obstructions to give a fair chance to the pilot and passenger.

It took a while to get the captain into the airplane. He had a small bag and his M-l. I got the engine started, taxied to where we could take off, poured the coal to the engine, and we were moving along. I waited as long as I could to pull the stick back, but I could tell that we were not fast enough and were running out of space.

I could see that we were going to hit the ridge ahead if I did not abort the takeoff and try to land where I was, but I was really too high for a landing. That did not sink in until it was too late; we were too high, and we did not have enough speed. We were caught in a kind of updraft thing, now called *wind shear*, and hit the ground very hard as I could not control the landing.

Suddenly, I was in a lot of pain and it took a few seconds to realize that I needed to get out of my seat and make sure there was not going to be a fire. I could see no fire, but there is always that danger. Somehow, I managed to get out of the airplane and tried to get the captain out.

My passenger was bleeding badly from his nose and face from when he had hit the fire extinguisher and knocked it loose, his face impacting the prong mount. He was out cold and not moving, but I managed to get to him and pulled his head up from the fire extinguisher. He was just coming to, and I managed to get the seat belt uncoupled and pull him up and out of his seat. We both tumbled backwards out of the plane, down the hill we had landed on, and rolled away from the airplane in case of explosion.

We were unable to climb up the hill after coming down in some very uneven terrain, like the top of a Chinese grave. I am not sure just how long we lay there until we got some help, but help was at hand, and before long, many local Chinese helpers came running to attend to us. That was one thing about China, there were always plenty of people around eager to help.

The locals had built our airstrips and barracks, and they were always available for loading and unloading, so help was never too far away. We were both in a great deal of pain, and one of the helpers offered me morphine, which I was afraid to accept as we had heard of thieves emptying the vials and filling them with something else.

We were helped over to a makeshift litter of some sort, but it would not do for two big Americans. We learned that they wanted us in a protected area as there were Japanese enemies all around us, who would have heard the airplane hit the ground and come running, so we had to be moved out of that area as quickly as possible or be captured. Our helpers wanted to move us immediately.

My back was broken, and I was in great pain, but the litter they brought just could not be used because I was just too big to fit on one of their litters. After a while, they came back carrying a big door they had located somewhere. I later learned it was the door off a local temple that they took because it was the biggest flat surface they could find, since most Chinese huts didn't have doors, but they finally got me on it and moved me out of that area and into a mud-walled hut.

The man in charge said that they had already radioed Y-Forces for help and it would arrive presently, but for now, the weather had already closed us in, which meant we would be there for a while. We laid there for three or four days, doing the best we could without medical help. A local doctor did help my pain with acupuncture, which was an unknown treatment but worked. While we were recovering, I told them there was a way to rebuild their landing area if they would make a few changes so that we could get to Paoshan more easily.

After a few days, the captain was up and walking around, but I was still confined to my door bed. On the third or fourth day, we could hear our L-5s coming after us, and as they approached, here came the helpers who had rescued us. They wanted to take us out and show us their newly rebuilt air strip! They had followed my ideas to a T, and now we knew that we had a short field take-off strip here, and that it might just work.

We waited, and sure enough, two L-5s came circling to land, which they did. By now, my passenger was in pretty good shape, I was surprised to see, and we made the transfer the next day and flew back to Kunming, where our hospital was located.

I spent a week or so in that hospital before being sent on to spend time fully recuperating at the 19th Liaison Headquarters. I had compression injuries to my vertebrae, and while recuperating in this larger MASH operation with more mud walls not too far from Kunming, I decided to get out of this chicken outfit and get into some real flying machines.

I requested transfer to the 27th Troop Carrier Squadron based at Yunnanyi (Yunnan). They accepted my transfer, for they had lost 15 aircraft a few weeks before and needed replacement pilots immediately.

This squadron was in the Yunnan Province, and since I already knew this terrain, I was a real help to them as they dropped supplies and equipment by parachute into the very same remote areas that we had gone into with the L-5's. But now I would be flying in on C-47s, and a C-47 is a much larger ship than a Stinson L-5 and carries up to 7,000 pounds of transport.

An L-5 Sentinel refueling at Baoshan, 1944. National Archives

CHAPTER 6

THE 27TH TROOP CARRIER SQUADRON

The 27th Troop Carrier Squadron was, of course, a much larger operation, and I was glad to be one of them and happy to be there.

Yunnani was a small village south of Kunming, situated in-between two of the highest ridges of the Eastern Himalayas. It has existed since the 13th Century, and our living quarters were built by hand of straw bricks. There were plenty of local eggs, and sometimes pigs from the market.

Our mission was to drop much-needed supplies by air to the embedded troops. Our supplies fell like manna from heaven, so long as we did not get shot down or crash into a mountain. Flying supplies across China may not sound glamorous, but because of the efforts of the Hump Pilots, over 650,000 tons of critically needed cargo and supplies were delivered to the Allies and Chinese, who were fighting the Japanese enemy to keep them out of China.

You had to pass a rigorous instrument flying test and have nerves of steel to join the 27th, because most of our flying would be in perilous weather, sometimes at night. When making an airdrop, there are different techniques depending on the terrain you are in, the weather, and the kind of cargo you drop.

Heavy cargo, like big armaments, 55-gallon tanks of gasoline, or barrels of cement, needed two parachutes, and sometimes a parachute would fail to open. If the plane we were flying gasoline in crashed, the gas would explode on impact. It was a dangerous game we played.

Sometimes, on takeoff or landing, the Chinese peasants ran in front of your plane because they believed it cut off the evil spirits chasing them. Slamming on the brakes of a fully loaded C-47 is not a good idea.

There were many fine pilots in our organization. Dominick Divincenzo, "Divi," we called him, was one of the best pilots I ever flew with. We had been together on the Mariposa, and he was a great guy. Divi had met many of the families in Kunming and befriended them, they were the ones who most likely went to Taiwan before the Communist takeover.

We all made many dangerous trips together. We flew many missions from Peishiyi (Baishiyi), our base near Chungking (Chongqing). From there, we rallied forth as far north as Hsian (Xi'an), also near the Mongolian border, and Hangchung (Hangcheng) in Shensi Province.

It may not be the stuff of Hollywood movies, transporting war supplies in a drafty plane, but with the food, medicine, and arms we dropped, we did our part to fight off the advance of an enemy that was as brutal and determined as any you can imagine, and so I was proud to join the Hump-T-Dumps (our unofficial name for our outfit).

We landed at larger airfields to pick up troops, soldiers in need of medical attention, heavy equipment, and sometimes even animals. So, there we were, just doing our thing, not killing anyone, but helping many by delivering life-saving medical supplies, ammunition, and food to those in need.

We stopped and spent the night at Hangchung. This was the town that had at least a thousand sweepers, who got up at the crack of dawn to sweep the whole town—a human street cleaner system. This was also where the very tall Chinese are from, and they were not friendly to Chiang Kai-shek.

All in all, it was much like things were back in the days of the emperors in China. We were warned not to venture into town unescorted or unarmed, but despite this warning, we went into town anyway. We were aware of this so-called problem, and we were sober and on good behavior.

Of course, no one was running up and putting lei around our necks; but on the other hand, no one was rude to us either. It was probably the cleanest city I had seen in China. The people there seemed to have a higher standard of living. All in all, it was fascinating.

Cairo, Egypt, May 1945
Standing: Lt. Eugene Trent, Lt. Francis Julliet, Lt. Robert Binzer.
Seated: Lt. Bernard Powers

CHAPTER 7

JINGBAO!

The story I'm telling now is the story as I recall it of one of my missions east of our base in Chungking, just south of Kunming in Yunnan province. The most frequented base out east was the Suichuan (Sichuan) airbase, and because of the constant danger of Japanese bombers requiring fighter escort, it had been decided the future missions to those airfields would be at night, with no lights or radios.

We had already done several successful missions like this, however, there were other problems with flying at night. One big problem was the Japanese Air Raids. Another problem going into these bases was that you were close enough to Japanese bases to expect raids by their bombers. This was still a very bad area for flying at night, and it was common to run into night Air Raids.

I remember being on the ground in my first Air Raid, and when the bombs started dropping, I ran like Hell for the Slit Trench, but it turned out to be in the opposite direction of the way I was running.

As I mentioned earlier, our fighters were able to provide air cover during daytime operations, but not at night, so we were on our own. Still, we had made many trips to this base, carrying bombs, ammunition, and gasoline in 55-gallon drums. Technically, it was surrounded, however, the Chinese guerillas maintained contact with the enemy and kept them some distance from these bases.

The instruction to make a high approach was always in the back of your mind. Making a low approach could mean small arms fire on your final approach, so we went in high and hoped for no air raids. I only made one daylight trip across this area, and we were eight or nine and in loose formation, with fighter cover both top and bottom.

The night missions were in an evenly spaced separation of about 15 or 20 minutes apart, without any fighter cover. At the time, we thought the Japanese had no night fighters, but we later found out that they did have some night fighters out there after all. It was not unusual to be caught in Suichuan during an air raid. If you were on the ground, you had only to find a place to hide, but in the air, as you were approaching Suichuan, you were instructed to go northeast and circle.

Now, this was at night, remember, and there is no place darker on this earth than war-torn China at night. All lights were extinguished so the bombers could not find a target, and the airfield turned off all lights and radio equipment so the enemy could not home in on our radios. So, we flew at night with no lights and used radio only in an emergency. As we approached Suichuan one night, the call went out,

"Jingbao! (Air Raid) Go northeast and circle!"

Fine, remember we are now using the fuel intended for our return trip. Remember how dark it is out there, and that there are many other C-47's out there, too, with no lights and no radio like us. Now it was sweat time! You had no idea where the others were, and you had no idea how long this circle maneuver would go on.

Another night, we made the trip and landed at Suichuan. While the aircraft was being unloaded, we went to the mess hall about two miles away for dinner. We returned to our aircraft after eating and made preparations for the return trip to the airbase at Chichiang (Zhejiang). After checking everything, I started the engines and notified the tower we were ready to taxi. No response.

As we turned out of the revetment and taxied out toward the runway, I called again. Then, out of the corner of my eye, I saw a red flare fired from the tower, which was often done when a ship needed to abort landing or takeoff. Here I was, near the end of the runway, with lights *on* and landing light *on*, ready to get onto the runway, when over the radio, we heard,

"Get out of there, it's a Jingbao (Air Raid)!"

Al Joyce, my co-pilot, cut the engines and lights and we hopped out of that C-47 faster than you can imagine.

Out across the rice paddies we went, running, no lights, not knowing where in hell I was running to, but trying to get as far from the runway and our C-47 as I could get.

After hiding out for some time, the sirens started again, along with lights on and a green flare, and we knew it was over. The bombers, if there were any, either thought we were fighters going up after them or they couldn't find us in the dark, or for some other reason left the area and did not drop anything on that trip. So, we finally got off the ground and back to Chichiang.

On another occasion in Suichuan, bombs were dropped while we were eating in the mess hall. We ran out to our bird after the ALL-CLEAR and found pieces of small incendiary or personnel bombs near our ship, but close inspection showed no damage to our aircraft, so on we went.

Perhaps one of the most terrifying few minutes for me was one night during an air raid. While circling, I was straining my eyeballs looking out into the black, hoping no other ship was near, when suddenly I saw two blue exhaust flames coming straight at us! I pushed down on the nose and grabbed the UHF radio mic, but radio silence, remember?

I knew that if we did not get some sort of separation established, we could lose some more people and aircraft. No one answered, and soon it was all over, so we proceeded to land at Suichuan. That's the way it was at times, and after it is over and you get your color back, you hope there will be no more such excitement today, or tomorrow.

Chinese soldier guarding line of Flying Tigers P-40 fighters,
Kunming, China, 1942. National Archives

CHAPTER 8

CHRISTMAS MISSION

It was planned for a choir to sing at a service for Christmas. Tom Quigley and I signed up for the choir and we had attended a couple of rehearsals. We were looking forward to the concert, but were disappointed to learn that we would be on detached service at another base located at Chanyi (Zhanyi), just northeast of Kunming.

We took off and arrived at Chanyi, where we found out we were to carry Chinese troops up north to Chengtu, where our B-29s staged out of. These Chinese soldiers needed to be flown back north to help the 14th Air Force protect their air bases, which were north of our location, and we had flown this route many times. The only problem was that we had no parachutes for our passengers, as required by regulation.

We raised our concerns, but we were told to go ahead and take all the Chinese with us, regardless of parachutes. This we did, and fortunately we had no problems this trip, so we were never faced with the problem of what to do with the Chinese IF we had been forced to bailout. But it was always on our minds. Now, the troops were loaded up, all seats filled, and the floor was also filled with as many soldiers as possible, shoulder-to-shoulder. None had parachutes. If any of them had ever flown before, it was in one of our transports.

Our own parachutes were carefully removed from the rear of the airplane and placed in the forward compartment, where the radio operator was located. We were not too happy to be flying 50 or 60 non-English speaking armed soldiers, all seated behind us, blocking the doorway and all carrying rifles. We assumed no ammunition, but we didn't ask them.

So, this was to be our Christmas mission—no singing in a choir, no cookies, and not a mission we would have selected on our own, but the trip went well, except for the mess in the back, where several of the Chinese soldiers got air sick. After we unloaded our passengers and got the plane cleaned up, we returned to Chanyi to pick up another full load of Chinese soldiers, also without parachutes, to take up north, and we made another round trip.

It was not the best Christmas ever, but we did get a Christmas ration of a six-pack of beer, and maybe a bottle of whiskey issued to us upon our return from the first trip north. At that point, after returning from the mission, we learned that our squadron was to be moved to another base closer to Kunming.

We would now call Chungking our new home base and would fly our missions out of that base, south of Kunming, just beyond the lake. After our service at Chanyi ended, we flew into our new location at Chungking, where I found that I shared a room with only three, instead of the four in a room like we had at Yurmani (Yurman).

Christmas Card from China

CHAPTER 9

DOG FIGHT ON
THE SALWEEN FRONT

The first main obstacle we had to overcome when we dropped supplies of all kinds to our troops embedded with the Chinese ground troops was avoiding the Japanese. We knew that they were holed up somewhere in a mountain hideout beside the Burma Road. We knew that this area was protected by Japanese fighters, and that we should avoid it, but there was no other way around. That mountain was in our way, whichever direction we came from.

Our bombers had made many runs at that mountain, and every effort was made to find some way to destroy their encampment and get them out of those mountains, but they were so far back and so well hidden that, up till now, it had been impossible to get a good shot at them.

After many failed attempts, our engineers tried a different tactic and drilled holes deep enough into the rock to set a big enough charge that would blow up the entire mountain and take care of that problem. However, this took a long time since it had to be done secretly, but finally, after months of hardship and hard hand labor, this risky and dangerous mission was done, and BOOM, the whole mountain was blown sky high.

When the smoke finally cleared and we got in there, we found out that there were not only Japanese soldiers inside but also women workers, tons and tons of food, and ammo of all kinds, like an underground city. If our engineers had not blown up the mountain, the Japanese enemy could have stayed in there indefinitely and caused us no end of problems.

But even after their mountain was gone, it was still a very dangerous area to be in as the Japanese were still encamped around there, and it was impossible to tell among the locals who was on their side and who was on ours. Still, we had no choice, and ran many missions from that place.

One attack nearly cost us all our lives. We were flying a drop mission to Longling, which was a little way from Paoshan, when we were attacked while waiting for the fighter escorts to arrive. Our squadron commander had asked for fighter cover because there was activity in this area and we were promised fighter cover.

When the mission got underway, I was flying as co-pilot for Captain William Peters, who was one of our more experienced pilots. We were scheduled for an airdrop west of Paoshan, close to the border of Burma, at Longling. This was an area in which Japanese fighters had recently been spotted, which was unusual. For quite some time before this, there had been no sign of enemy fighters. So, this trip we would fly with a fighter escort. Since our C-47 was slower than the P-38s, we staggered departure times.

Due to their speed and our slowness, we took off 12 minutes before them and planned to meet up over the Paoshan area. We departed as planned and flew ahead to wait for the fighters, who would follow and provide cover while we flew to our target. We arrived at the rendezvous area over Paoshan and started to circle, awaiting the arrival of the fighters.

Captain Peters noted that the weather in the direction we were headed was weathered in; it looked like a line of thunderstorms coming out of the west. He was sure that the fighter escorts could not, or would not, go follow us into the storm, and felt that it was best for us to go on ahead and get to the target because circling now would only waste precious gasoline. I was quick to agree that we should go on ahead, which we did.

We set our aircraft up for turbulent weather. The wheels were lowered, speed was reduced, and our seats were lowered to the lowest notch. We removed our headsets and tightened our seat belts, and I think we added a little carburetor heat. Sure enough, soon the weather was the worst we could have imagined. We had flown into a full-blown thunderstorm.

It was the worst storm I had ever been in. The first updraft sent us up way too far to be flying without oxygen. Then, suddenly, we were in a downdraft, all accompanied by extreme turbulence. It was most unsettling.

As I stated, we had taken our headsets off when we entered the storm because they would have been in the way and useless. So, when we finally flew out of the storm, we were unable to hear what was going on over the radio; however, our radio operator was listening for us, and just as we flew into the storm, he yelled at us to put our headsets back on immediately, as there was big trouble behind—a dog fight!

We listened as we let down to drop our load. The weather at the drop zone was clear but surrounded by the high clouds. We kept listening as we flew the drop mission, and when we heard what was going on, we realized that if we had we stayed in our circling pattern a little longer, we would have been in the middle of that battle that was now going on behind us.

Our fighter cover had arrived, and a huge air battle was going on directly behind us on our return route to Yunnanyi and home. We finished our drop mission and headed back to base, but only after flying north for about 10 minutes, this time staying close to the cloud cover so that we could jump into them if we spotted any enemy fighters. Fortunately, we made it back to our base without further incident.

We were very happy about having missed the big excitement, but what we did not know at the time and did not see while circling the airfield at Paoshan, because our eyes were looking for our fighter cover, was that several C47s from another squadron were directly below us on the ground, unloading Chinese soldiers.

Their activity was probably what had brought the Japanese fighters into this area, but they were just too busy going after the ground targets and avoiding our P-38s, which engaged them after they met while arriving at Paoshan to either cover us, go after one of our fighters, or chase us.

When one of the Japanese fighters was hit, the pilot aimed the crippled plane at a C47 that was on the ground, unloading the Chinese soldiers. The damaged Japanese fighter crashed into one of the C-47s, which both caught fire and burned. It took three months for the fighter squadron to clean up that area we had just been in. As we worked our way south down into Burma, we were relieved by the 10th Air Force and glad of it.

Relaxing at Chung King
Back Row (L-R): Lt. Bernard Powers, Major John Caldwell, Lt. Chuck Statton, Lt. Albert Joyce, Lt. Thomas Quigley, *Front Row (L-R)*: Lt. C.W. Taylor, Lt. Robert Binzer

CHAPTER 10

TROOP CARRIER MISSION 5: UP A RIVER WITHOUT A TAIL

On or about November 13, 1944, my buddy Albert Joyce, who I flew many missions with, and I were assigned to temporary duty at Peishiyi (Baishiyi) Airfield, which was then a small town just west of Chungking. At that time, Peishiyi Airfield was home to Chiang Kai-shek's Chinese Airforce 4th Pursuit Group, and now the 14th Airforce was there as well. There were several small airstrips around Peishiyi that we sometimes used as well.

Our assignment that day was to provide assistance transporting personnel, mail, and general freight, both out of and into Peishiyi and other bases in the northern regions of the China near the Mongolian border, which was a dangerous area as it took us closer to the enemy. We left our base in a C-47 aircraft #293759, I believe it had the tail letters *AF*.

Today, we were transporting mail up from Yunnani back to Chungking. Onboard was our crew, Crew Chief Sgt. Clifford Spiegelberg and Radio Operator Sgt. Bob Omara. Weather was routine, we were "On Top" flying at about 12,000 feet and the weather at Peishiyi Airfield was reported as overcast with reported visibility one mile. We were letting down over the Peishiyi beacon, when suddenly, a strange voice came on the frequency, announcing:

"Amelican Dog! Amelican Dog!"

We realized that we had picked up another station on the Peishiyi Airfield frequency, a station we did not want to be on. Did they know we were there? But breaking out of the overcast, we could not see the field directly below as we should have. Maybe it was a visibility problem? With visibility about half a mile or less, this was either the worst case of stupidity or we weren't sure what else.

It was probably the fog on top of the clouds, but in any case, conditions were such that we would have to letdown at Peishiyi on instruments. Letting down on instruments was the worst scenario imaginable. But wait, this was not the only problem at this base! Here, we not only had a very poor letdown procedure, but we also had the Japanese harassing us on our letdown frequency, so we didn't know if they had somehow screwed up the letdown direction signal, or worse.

Finally, we could see the field below and realized that visibility was not one mile, as we had been told, but closer to a quarter-mile due to the dense fog in the valley. We had some trouble finding the runway but arrived at our destination in spite of the clandestine radio signals. This note was filed away for future reference:

Beacon at Peishiyi unreliable due to enemy intervention, and weather reporting not accurate.

We landed on the short runway there with no problem, and while our drop was being unloaded, we went to get lunch. When we came back to the plane, we found that our load for the next day also included a few passengers for Chungking and various packages, and, oh yes, in the load going back to Peishiyi would be barrels containing 300 pounds of cement.

Now, we had to consider the weight of our load and decided to stay over for the night because the airport at Chungking was very interesting[5]—it had been carved out of the side of a mountain at about 300 feet or so above the Yangtze River.

There was no "going around" here—if you had to abort your landing, you had better do it early as the runway ended against a mountain. On departure, you took off in the opposite direction, no matter which way the wind was blowing. Remembering our last trip to Peishiyi and the fog, we decided to stay the night.

The weather out of Yunnanyi the next morning was no problem, but checking the weather at Peishiyi, we found

---

[5] This airfield may be what was then called the Winter Airfield strip, right next to the Yangtze. It may have also been referred to as Bishan.

that we would have to make another instrument approach on that same mysterious radio beacon we just got off of, which we weren't too keen on. Considering the weight of our load, this airport would be tricky.

The weather people there had not really seen good visibility for so long that they often reported one-mile visibility, when, in fact, you would have to argue about it being one mile. This was scary, but as we studied the charts, we saw that we could take another route that took us up the river and brought us out into the valley at Peishiyi.

Taking this route meant we could fly underneath the overcast, which was then about 200-300 feet above the Yangtze river, to slip into the valley and hop over to the landing strip at Chungking. No problem!

So, on the morning of November 14, 1944, we departed Chungking, headed up the river toward the airfield for Peishiyi. We made a right turn out, descending to allow more space from the overcast above. As we were about to level out, 200-300 feet above the river, we suddenly noticed several cable wires directly in our path!

It all happened so fast. Al tried to go under them, and we missed all but one, but suddenly we hit something, and all hell broke loose. The plexiglass navigator's dome was smashed, and Al calmly commented, "No Rudder!" and wrestled for control of the plane.

We could not turn now, and there were huge mountains all around us. The river turned, but we, of course, could not turn with it. Without a rudder, we were unable to control the plane and had reached a point where the Yangtze changes course, with mountains all around. Al was yelling at me to help him hold up the left wing and telling me he could not hold it up by himself as we skimmed very low across the countryside. I could see that we narrowly missed a bamboo tree by inches.

We increased power to maintain altitude, and, realizing the seriousness of the situation, I yelled at everyone to prepare to bail out. However, as everyone went to the rear of the plane to get their parachutes and get ready to jump, we had problems maintaining level flight. Then, Al said, "Call them back, I can't hold the tail up," and so I did.

They all came running back to the bulkhead. Al asked me for help in holding up the left wing as it took nearly full aileron control to manage the wings at a level position and level things out.

We increased power to keep what altitude we had, but we were heading straight for a mountain, so Al asked me to go to full left throttle and cut back a little on the right engine. It worked! By increasing and decreasing power on opposite engines, we were able to navigate the mountains, just skimming the tops of some bamboo trees, and continued to follow the course of the river.

Having lost most of the controls, both pilots were required to manhandle the left-wing aileron to maintain level flight. As we breezed across this area of trees, I could see an island dead ahead of us, a grass field that had been a former American Volunteer Group (AVG) airfield.

I immediately informed Al that there was the field we would have to land in.

There was no other choice for us, and we were at the wrong altitude, but we did have to try and make a landing at this place off to our side. I asked Al if he wanted the wheels down. "Yes," he said, "but don't lock them."

We were too fast due to our loss of lift, which we did not yet fully comprehend, but Al made a fine recovery. We hit the ground hard on the main gear, bounced once or twice, and started a long slow skid or ground loop, probably due to our ground speed. Finally, with both of us on the brakes, we skidded to a stop, and I locked the gear down.

Wow! We had done it; we had nursed this big bird to a halt. We could hardly believe it. Finally, we were down, and with no injuries. Scared out of our wits and with wobbly knees, we managed to all pile out to see what we had by the tail and inspect the damage to the ship.

Oh golly! Probably the first shocker was that there was no rudder at all! You could see where the rudder had been, but it was completely missing. No sign of our rudder anywhere!

In fact, 10-12 inches of the vertical stabilizer was also missing, most of the top side antennae was gone, and the left deicer had been caught in the cable too and was damaged at the tip end of the left wing with a split down the middle, making a nice spoiler. So, this was the reason we had no lift from the left wing.

Upon inspecting the support at the center of the windshields, we found a large dent, indicating where the cable had first come into contact with us. Fortunately for us, it had bounced or slid along enough to tear along the upper surface of the fuselage and do its damage there, instead of splitting open the cockpit and fuselage like a can of sardines, with the obvious consequences. But thank God, we were all unharmed, with no scratches or injuries.

We were lucky, very lucky. Yes, someone above was looking over us. Now all we had to do was find a way out of this mess. Bob Omara had Ed Martin, our radio operator, unreel the trailing antenna for some distance, and we found a willing volunteer, a Chinese soldier, to hold the end high as possible off the ground so that Bob could get the HF radio working long enough to contact operations at our base in Chungking to tell them what had happened and explain our predicament, our location, and what was needed.

They advised us to stand by, questioned everyone as to what was needed to put the airplane back in flying condition, and said they would get back to us soon. To our surprise, when we checked back later that day, they informed us that a crew made up of the finest aircraft mechanics in the Corps would fly in early the next morning and see if they could get this bird repair and back in the air.

We got help from the Chinese that were there to unload the barrels of cement, and sure enough, the next morning as promised, here came Captain Cooney, Lt. Cormier, Sgts.

Burk, Barkalow, Brewer, and others, and they had all the parts we needed to put everything back together.

Getting spare parts in the middle of China was next to impossible as everything had to be shipped in, but our recovery crews salvaged crashed planes and reused the parts. There were so many crashed planes along the China Hump that it was nicknamed "the Aluminum Trail," so there was an ample supply of parts. Some of these wrecks are still there.

After final repairs, the bird was back in flying order. After offloading the barrels of cement, we returned to Peishiyi and continued our assigned route to the northern bases of Chengtu, Nanchong, Liangshan, and Xian.

All this happened over 50 years ago, and just last year, another story came out about those cables. We were not the only ones to hit them—another C-47 heading in the opposite direction hit them, too. The airfield at Chunking had no authorized instrument approach because of its location, and the pilots in this plane were forced to fly below the cliffs on the riverbanks due to bad weather.

When this crew came upon our same cables, they had to make an instantaneous decision whether to pull up into the clouds and risk hitting a mountain or go low and try and get under the cables, like we did. They chose the latter course, but not soon enough, and the bottom cable scraped along the top of the plane, removing the radio antennas and the top half of their vertical stabilizer and rudder.

These two factors compounded one another, and when they arrived on the airstrip, they could not contact the tower. On their first pass to the strip, they found they could not turn very well with half the rudder gone, so they almost collided with the tower, scaring the operators half to death. The second time around, they made a larger circuit and successfully landed.

Nobody knew that it was the Chinese who had strung these cables because this is the same way the Japanese bombers flew in undetected to make sneak attacks on Chungking.

Chungking was once the most bombed city outside of London, and the Cable Trap was one of the best-kept secrets in China, and nearly cost many lives. It was a ride like no other, and not one to be forgotten.

Compadres (L-R) Lt. Robert Binzer, Lt. Al Joyce

CHAPTER 11

THE LIANGSHAN B-29S

We flew direct to Peishiyi to get our assignment, which took us up north to the B29 base in Liangshan, then up to an airfield that had some of the smaller air strips supporting the emergency landing areas for the B-29 Bombers.

This was up in the Sichuan province, but there was a problem at the first or second small airfield we stopped at. I can't remember which airstrip it was, maybe it was Luliang or Nanchong, but I'll never forget the sight.

Our first trip into that area was something to remember. It was a clear day, and you could see forever as we were letting down into the valley below. Looking down, I spotted a crashed B-29 down in a rice paddy, then I spotted another and another. I pointed them out, and we all looked.

Below us, we could see perhaps eight or nine B-29s scattered all over the valley floor. One glance at the airfield below where we were to land, and we counted four more.

Two of the B-29s had collided head-on at the end of the air strip, and the third had stopped short, just short of the others. The other one had made it off the strip and onto the grass.

We had room to land short and found a place to park away from the wrecks without a problem, but when we landed, we discovered that the crews on the ground thought we were a hospital ship coming for the injured, of which there were many laying around, moaning, and many dead as well.

This had all happened the night before returning from a bombing mission to Japan. Each of the B-29s ran out of fuel for some reason—probably the strong head winds—and one by one, they tried to make it into the field, which could accommodate one B-29, empty.

So, in the dark, the first three had made it in, but the fourth, unable to stop, slammed into the #3 ship head-to-head. The remaining ships could not make it to the field, and hearing the commotion, had no choice but to belly in the rice paddies.

At night, this is really not a nice thing to consider. Yes, they could have bailed out, but having wounded and dead crew on board, they had no other choice but to try to land.

Most were damaged in some way, either shot up or in bad condition due to crashing. One of the bombers had lost a tail gunner because the Japanese enemy had bullets that went right through the bullet proof glass on the tail guns.

We had no litters on our aircraft, but we assured the folks there that we would stand by until the hospital ship arrived with medics.

It was a sad sight, seeing all those B-29s scattered around like toys, all crashed in different angles and conditions. Inspecting the two wrecks that had collided on the strip, we learned that one tail gunner was killed, as the enemy evidently had 20mm shells that could penetrate our "Bullet Proof Glass."

This episode made quite an impression on me, so much so that when we arrived back home and I was told that I could go right into B-29 training, I remarked that I did not think that would be what I wanted to do just then.

Our next destination that evening was a base called Sian. This was up in the country where the Chinese Communists were strong, and we were informed to only go in twos or threes, armed and together for our own protection.

After seeing all the crashed B-29s lying around, we were very glad to make the drop and get out of that area as fast as we could.

Crashed C46 near Liangshan China. National Archives

CHAPTER 12

THE ABLE QUEEN

Here is the story of the Able Queen, a brand new C-47B that we had to abandon one dark and cold night in February 1945. I have told this story before, but you often think back on the little details of something that could have been overlooked at the time of writing up the story for the book. So, here is what I remember now. Somehow, I think it was on the 9th of February, destination Chichiang.

Chichiang was sort of a "jumping off" base. Bombers and fighters were based there, and our job was to help keep the base supplied with gasoline, ammunition, and other supplies, like parts and just about anything we could carry in a C-47. We had made many of these trips to the east because the enemy had been driven out of the western part of China, and we were no longer needed to support the ground troops there.

Now, it was time for us to concentrate on the eastern and south-eastern parts of China. Chihchiang was important because it was not surrounded by the enemy, as were the bases out east, so going to and from Chihchiang was not a real "sweat deal" like the others; the weather in the winter there was tricky. From the Chihchiang base, we would occasionally fly on to one of two or three bases in southeast China, taking the same sort of supplies to them.

The only problem was that these bases were located in the part of China that had very recently been occupied by the Japanese enemy. But with the aid of the Chinese guerillas, we were able to keep these bases in operation. Fighters would land, top off their tanks, take on ammo or bombs, and get right back out to the coast, and/or Formosa, to strike the shipping or other targets. On the way home, they would stop there again and get enough fuel to return to their bases.

We had no weather service as we have today. In fact, there were pitifully few real weather stations in the whole of China. So, there was always a concern about the weather, no matter where you flew. To make matters worse, due to the shortage of gasoline, we were only allowed enough fuel to get there and get back home, with twenty or thirty minutes of reserve in your tanks.

Our ship, the Able Queen, was not the original ship of that name. This was a new aircraft, more or less, brought in with the replacements for lost planes that we received into the squadron. This was a C-47B Skytrain, equipped with two-stage blower superchargers. That's the only way we could have made it to 22,000 feet.

Pilot discretion could often be used to request extra fuel, if reasonable need could be established, but sometimes that was a real hassle. Needless to say, this situation sharpened your skills at navigation immeasurably. These were the conditions we had to deal with while in China at that time.

Our mission today was to take a load of gasoline to Chihchiang and return to Chungking. No problem! Our crew:

Field Engineer: George Youngling

RO: Dan Anderson

Co-Pilot: Warren C. Elliott

Pilot: Bob Binzer

I don't recall where we left from for sure, but I believe it was Kunming, where we were loaded before taking off for Chihchiang.

Weather in February 1945 was not the best, but I don't recall any great concern about weather as we departed. It was up on top and away we go! Checkpoint came up ahead of schedule, and the beacon at Chihchiang was loud and clear. We landed in fairly good weather, but to beat the weather, we had to move fast. So, instead of going to the mess hall as we had usually done, we decided to stay with the ship and ask for full fuel on our trip back because the headwinds were strong.

While refueling, Warren and I ran to the local diner, the "McDonald's of the day," which was not McDonalds at all. To save time, we got some hamburgers as we wanted to get ahead of the weather that we felt was developing. We had requested full tanks, which was asking a lot and required special permission. But we knew we had head winds to fight on our return and faced the possibility of some icing in the clouds.

Not too many days prior to this trip, we had lost two aircraft and crews due to icing conditions. So, we knew that it was possible to encounter icing and that our C-47 could not handle it. I was determined to avoid icing, if it was at all possible, so we stayed on top as we started our trip home.

While Warren and I went up the street for the food and ate, George stayed behind and took care of the fuel. We brought food back for him, but when we came back with his food, we found out that we had been refused additional gasoline.

After much hassle, they reluctantly allowed us more fuel, but only after the base commander okayed our request because he too realized that the winds were building up. Finally, we were off for points West. I think we were going back to Kunming, perhaps to Chungking, I can't really recall where now. But by now, we had weather, so we climbed to the top. It took a long time, and we topped out at perhaps 16 or 18-thousand feet.

The tops continued to build, and we rose to 20-thousand, and then finally 22-thousand feet to get above the weather. We had been on oxygen for some time now, but for the first hour, I was not concerned.

We would check our checkpoint off to the north—to Guiyang. It was soon dark, and it took a long time to reach our radio checkpoint at Kweiyang. It appeared off our right wing, as it should have. However, this went on for another hour. Our radio indicated that we were on course to Chungking, which was our base north of Kunming.

Again, we checked on the ADF, and Kweiyang (Guiyang) was still at 90 degrees. This was not good because it should now be indicating behind that point at perhaps 100 or 115 degrees. This went on for many hours, trying to reach Kunming. We had reduced our power, setting to a minimum flow setting to conserve gasoline and stay in the air as long as possible, but this also reduced our forward track as well, if there was any forward track at all.

We had flown out our ETA and just kept getting higher and higher. Now, we were still on oxygen to stay above the weather and were getting more than a little concerned. At this point, I began to doubt our checkpoint, but the Kunming beacon and Chichiang beacon were still providing the proper bearings of:

: .linl.li Ql 1111 11 7—nuij III li

So, we continued to bore on through the night. It was about 5 or 6 p.m. when we left Chichiang, so we had been in the dark for quite a while, with the checkpoints still showing as before. There had to be something wrong with the ADF or the station north of us, we thought, but we were really standing still, as far as forward progress goes, although we really had no way to determine this back then.

All of this happened in the days before much was known about the jet stream. We were not usually flying at this altitude, so we had no real experience with the jet stream or being at this altitude. We didn't know that the jet stream had lowered now and was straight into us at that altitude at 170 mph, which, at times, gave us a zero-ground speed, but we had no way to measure it, nor any knowledge of it.

By now, we had reached our ETA for the Kunming area, and still had no significant change in our ADF response. We confirmed our suspicions that we were possibly in big trouble, so I asked Dan to request a bearing from a ground station, indicating that we were uncertain as to our location at this time. Had we been aware of what was happening, we could have returned to Chichiang and landed, but we certainly would not then have had this story to tell.

In addition, it was almost unheard of to scrub a mission due to winds. In this case, we would have been forgiven, but people seldom believe the truth when a mission is scrubbed (unless they, too, had been in that same weather).

The weather below was not good, and I don't recall our ever getting a bearing, or any help, from the ground station. We had been in the air now nearly eight or nine hours, flying on about six hours of fuel.

Finally, we realized that we would have to abandon ship and started making preparations before our final fuel ran out. Secret codes were destroyed, along with any charts with radio frequencies.

George had now reached the point of great concern. He was afraid that we were over Lake Kunming and that we would drown upon hitting the water. I did not think we were near Lake Kunming; however, I did not know where we were, and I could not see what difference it would make if we made a turn back to the east for a few minutes, as George had requested.

We reported this back to the ground station, and they were concerned that we would go screaming on east with this tailwind and wind up in enemy territory. Later, we learned that the ground stations were able to hear us, but we could not hear them. So, I turned east while everyone else on board began getting ready to go.

We knew what was supposed to be in our parachute backpack, but there was often something missing, and none of us had our very own parachute. We were using the parachutes that had been loaded on the airplane by someone else for our mission.

Warren and I began tearing up any papers that might be useful to the enemy. The little pieces we slipped out a window, piece by piece. This did not take too long. We may have taken a chart of the area that we were supposed to be in, but I am not at all sure about that right now.

We had a Thompson machine gun with a case of ammo, but no one wanted to take the machine gun along with them. I certainly did not. I decided to take all the medical supplies we could handle, and Andy and Warren took the flashlights and any food we had. I do not recall what George took with him.

We had no choice but to bail out of this nice new airplane. Dan radioed that we were about to abandon ship. It was not until later that I found out that he had gotten no confirmation of his message from our Operations Office back at Yunnanyi. But it wouldn't have mattered anyway because it was time to go. Now! No one seemed to be eager to be the first one.

Bail Out

The jump door panel was removed, and it was time to jump. We agreed to go out together, one after another, as close as possible so we might land near one another. The first one that was able was to build a bonfire for a rendezvous point. The ship was on autopilot, gear down with ¼-flaps to be slower for our jumping out, all lights ON—perhaps, I thought, to enable someone to avoid the inevitable crash.

No one was eager to be the first to leave. Finally, I mentioned that someone has to go—NOW. Suddenly, George, our crew chief, got up and bolted out the door, pulling his ripcord as soon as he reached the doorway. His chute opened and blew him back into the doorway, nearly to the door of the toilet, and then George was gone—his chute quickly following him out the door, except for the last little bit, which caught and trailed out the jump door. Oh, poor George! A piece had caught and was fluttering in the wind! A piece had ripped away from his chute.

This was a disaster, as it would seem. George would be injured or killed due to some of the parachute being missing. Oh, God! Please help him! To see him pulling his ripcord as soon as he reached the doorway was a shock; it was unbelievable.

George was gone, a piece of his parachute ripped away. I hollered to the rest to make dammed sure they were out the door before they pulled the ripcord. The plane was now on autopilot. We could run out of fuel at any moment. We quickly agreed that one must be out and away from the aircraft before pulling the ripcord.

Dan got to the door next and asked for a push as he went out, which I did. Then, Warren had to go. He also asked for the push, which I half-heartedly did as I was not at all sure that my push was any guarantee of getting him past the tail. Then, myself... only there was no one left to push me out. But it was now or never.

A push was not needed, of course, so I jumped clear and found myself falling, tumbling through the pitch-black night. I realized that I must now pull on that ripcord and get on with this business of surviving. When I was certain I was clear of the ship, I pulled the cord and—much to my relief—the parachute worked as it should have. There was a welcome jolt, and I thanked God for whatever help He had given me on that score.

We left our ship "On Top," and were soon in the clouds, below which, as we later we discovered, was freezing rain that we went through. My first recollection, it seems now, was the profound silence that was about me.

After thanking the Lord, I looked around. I could see the lights of our ship heading off in the distance, as both engines still had some fuel left. While quietly floating down to the cloud deck below, I watched the Able Queen disappear until I could no longer see her. I was sick about losing our beautiful Able Queen. However, the excitement at hand helped to keep this in the background of my mind for the time being.

We were coming down in a valley about 150 miles south of Kweiyang. It was very dark below; I must have been in the clouds, for I could see nothing at all. Then, I was aware that I was between two layers of clouds, and I couldn't believe how quiet it was.

There was no sensation of "going down"—just a slight swinging effect. At that time, I remembered to cross my ankles, as I had been taught, in case I came down across a fence or something. I crossed my ankles and peered down into the blackness below, remembering what I was taught about controlling oscillation on the way down.

Before long, I was out of the clouds and could see more as I peered down into the blackness below me—hoping to see on what, or where, I might be landing. The darkness grew blacker and blacker, and then, WHAM! I was now on the ground and didn't seem to be hurt. Again, I gave thanks. I still had that ripcord in my hand. I don't know why—you're not supposed to hold onto that thing, but for some reason, I still gripped it.

It was a surprise to me: I really expected the trip to the ground to last a little longer, but there I was. I realized my parachute was in a small tree of some kind, and I lay there for what seemed to be a long time, just looking around, realizing that I was not injured, and again giving thanks for that. But there was nothing to see. It was very dark and perhaps foggy.

My chute was caught in a small tree, and I laid there quietly, listening for anything that might be about, but heard nothing. I pulled out my .45 and threw a shell into the chamber, then replaced it into the shoulder holster.

At the same time, I said, but not too loudly, "Megwa Feege, Megwa Feege Bing," meaning, "I am an American airman, I am an American airman soldier."

No answer.

We really had no idea where we were, or if we were even in friendly territory. Then, I got up and wrestled my chute down, out of the tree, and balled it up under my arm as best I could. I put on my cap that had been tucked inside my flight jacket and looked around. It was pitch black now. I had no flashlight, and freezing rain was falling, so I decided to start walking.

I took about six to eight steps forward, and wham! I dropped about four or five feet into what I believed was a rice paddy—I never found out. This scared the daylights out of me! I had not expected it, so now I became more cautious. I realized that I was out in the freezing rain and my jacket was starting to get iced over.

I got up, started walking downhill, and hollered for Warren or Dan, since they should have been the closest ones to me. Pretty soon, I heard someone yelling faintly in the distance, and I answered them back. I couldn't tell who it was yet, but I started off in that direction and kept walking and yelling until I could hear him better. As we closed in on one another, I finally heard that it was Warren. Was I ever glad!

Finally, Warren, my co-pilot, and I found each other, and it was a great relief for us both. Warren was ok, too, and said he had passed a house up the way, and that maybe we should go back up there and see if they would let us in, out of the cold weather, and perhaps try to find out where we had landed.

I followed him, and he led me back up the path to where he had found a little house. The door was not a door as we know it, but a bamboo screen-like affair, stretched across a doorway that was open at the top and bottom. We knocked on the partition and tried our Chinese, mentioning that we were "Megwa Feege," but heard nothing—no response.

Warren shined his flashlight in, and what we saw was really scary. The family that lived there was plastered against the far wall, eyes wide open and with the most frightful look frozen on their faces that I have ever seen.

They were scared to death of us and were in complete shock. It was apparent right away that we were not going to make friends with this family under the present conditions.

We realized that they did not understand us and were afraid to come to the door, and we decided to leave them alone as we were afraid that, in their frightened condition, they might fire a gun, or something else, at us for protection. So, back into the freezing rain and down the path we went.

Finding Lost Crew Members

What to do? Well, I had noticed a stack of hay around a pole back down the path that Warren had found. We decided to go down and start a bonfire so the others might find us, as we had planned together to get a fire going to help find one another.

We set up one of the parachutes to cover our backs as a shelter and pulled some hay from the stack. Using matches from our survival packs, we got the fire going in front of us. It must have been cold as it had been freezing the rain that had fallen; however, I do not recall being cold. Regardless, the fire felt good and warmed our hands as we watched for someone to come to us and hoped they would be friendlies.

We let the fire get fairly large and kept watch for the others as far we could see downhill in the dark. Talking it over, we figured that I had landed farther up on this hill from where we were at that time, and that Warren must have landed not far from that house, back up the way behind that. So, it seemed logical that Dan, our radio operator, must have landed somewhere down below, and that George, our crew chief, landed somewhere even farther down the lane.

Poor George! We really worried about him because of what we had witnessed as he went out the door. He couldn't possibly have landed easily as I had done. Most likely, his was a very hard landing. We continued to watch and feed the fire from the stack behind us, and after about an hour, I thought I saw a light, very briefly.

Warren had seen it also, but then it disappeared again. We both thought we saw glimpses of a flashlight down below us. Being concerned about who it might be, I figured one of us should get the .45 out. I asked Warren to go up on a rise behind us and cover us with his .45 until we could see who was coming up the hill.

"No way, I can't hit the side of a barn with this thing. You go up there and cover me," Warren said.

Following his instruction, I went up in the tall grass behind where we had been and laid down with my .45 at the ready. We stayed that way for quite a while, with me laying on the ground about 10 or 20 feet uphill and behind Warren.

We saw the light again, and whoever it was, they were headed in our direction. Suddenly, about 1:30 or 2 a.m. in the morning, Dan appeared, flashing his light at us and letting us know it was him. We were so glad to see him! He told us that he had been watching us too but was cautious about walking up there without knowing who was sitting at the fire.

We kept that fire going and wondered what had become of George. We had witnessed his chute being damaged and knew instantly that he had gone down. However, not knowing how much damage a chute can take and still be useful, we had serious doubts as to George's condition. We decided it was best to wait until daylight to start looking for him. So, now there were three of us feeding the fire and watching downhill. This we did until it was starting to get light enough to where you could see where you were going. But then it began to snow again, heavier than before.

As soon as it was light enough to leave, we put out the fire and started down the path in the snow, going down the one that Dan had approached us on. We reasoned that George was somewhere out in that direction and could see another roadway farther down the valley, so we followed the path we were on toward the other road. Dan pointed to the area where he felt he had landed.

We decided that I had landed between Warren and Dan, and that George was somewhere below us, where that small roadway was. Warren, being somewhat lighter in weight, must have drifted farther up the slope of this mountain. We covered the ground pretty fast, going downhill, and could now see that there was a roadway of some type beyond.

As the path reached the roadway, we saw a small shack of some kind with three walls, open on the side toward the path. Inside, a lady was preparing food in what looked like a small dug-out log of some kind. She had a short pole and was beating and kneading a dough of some sort, something that looked like mashed potatoes but was most likely rice.

The lady was friendly and greeted us with smiles and gestures, indicating that we should come inside the building. She did not interrupt her work or seem to be the least bit afraid of us. She still seemed friendly as we began trying to inquire and converse with her using our pointy-talky book that had sentences in English on one side and the Chinese meaning written just opposite. But this was not working at all, for she clearly did not read Chinese.

Not understanding anything we pointed to, she still smiled very graciously, nodded, and offered us some food. We kindly refused the offer of food as we had no idea what it was or how it might affect our system, but we tried to find out which way we should go to find the nearest village.

She seemed to understand and indicated to our right, or up the valley. We tried to thank her as best we could and headed up the road. It was snowing hard by now, and it was beginning to be a fairly good snow, with large flakes but no wind.

We looked down the roadway again for any sign of George being down that road, but not a soul was to be seen, so we started our walk up this roadway, which was an unpaved, unmaintained, wide mountain path.

The snowfall got heavier now; the flakes were large. Luckily, the wind was very slight, so we were able to easily walk up the dirt road, crunching the fresh snow under our boots.

The Villagers

We had been walking for about an hour or so—I'm not sure how long it was we'd been walking before we realized that there were people following us. Behind us, there were at least 40-50 Chinese, mostly young people and children, following. They were so curious and aghast of these strange-looking people moving through their land. Silent, reserved, and wide-eyed, they followed closely behind us.

Some of the younger ones pointed to our shoes, especially my size 13 Paratrooper boots crunching through the snow, leaving tracks. They were extremely curious and kept pointing at my paratrooper boots while laughing and trying to hide. At least they seemed friendly enough, unlike the headhunters.

So, up the roadway we all went through the snow, us ahead and them following behind us. After perhaps an hour or so on the road, we began to see signs of a village, and the crowd following behind us had grown even larger than before.

For some reason, I turned around to look behind us and was astonished to see at least 200-300 people following behind us now. Each had the most curious look about them. We figured that we must have been the first foreigners they had ever seen in this remote area.

Soon after, we began to recognize the outskirts of a village on either side of the road. Finally, we reached what must have the center of a village, where we saw some sort of a reception committee standing in front of a building flying the Chinese flag.

What a relief! It was very reassuring to us because we still had no idea where we were, nor who these people were. But what a relief to see the Chinese, and not the Japanese flag flying. The natives were friendly enough, though, so we were not scared, as I recall. Anxious, yes, and despite being concerned about George, but we were not afraid of these natives.

As things happen, it so happened that they were having a funeral at the same time, for which the whole town had turned out. In Chinese funerals, the body is carried down the street and firecrackers are thrown on top of the coffin to ward off evil spirits.

While all of this was going on, a lady offered us some local food, but we did not know what it was and declined it. Then, she offered us a bowl of navel oranges covered by white powder. We didn't know what the powder was, but we were hungry, so we took them to eat and asked for more. They brought out a couple more, which we three split. We later found out that only the wealthiest people could have afforded oranges like these in the dead of winter because they came from occupied territory in the

North and had been preserved for several months with the white powder.

We walked on and I stopped in front of the person who was the most dressed-up of anyone there to greet them. He had a man with him, who, judging by his uniform, we guessed was a Chinese Army official. They were both standing out in front of the biggest building in town that flew a flag. They invited us into their building.

We entered and attempted to explain our situation and discuss our desires. No one there understood us, and nobody there spoke English. We pulled out the pointie-talkie books that we carried in our survival packs. These small booklets with English-Chinese translations were issued to airmen in case of bailout, but nobody there was able to read the Chinese printed in the booklets. They did not even recognize the Chinese flag.

Still, through gestures and drawings, we talked about our lost crew chief and pantomimed that he may have been injured and was out there in the snow somewhere. Again, we tried using the pointie-talkie books to communicate, and now they seemed to help a little, however, the dialect in our books did not appear to be a dialect that these people were used to.

Finally, the mayor of this village appeared at the building to greet us, and he seemed to understand our plight. He had a man with him who spoke a few words of English. We learned that there was a telephone in the building, an old hand-crank telephone like we used to have in the US in the 20s and 30s. The man told us they were getting an interpreter on the phone.

We found that attempting to talk to someone on their phone was nearly impossible. Nevertheless, I did feel that we were told that an English interpreter was on his way and would arrive in a few hours to help. In the meantime, the man who must have been the mayor offered to show us around town.

First, he took us to his house, which was quite large, and wanted us to meet his family too and show us all of the conveniences he had. Of everything I was shown, he was most proud of their bedroom set. It was of a Western design and quite nice.

After showing us his home and the rest of the village, we went back to the Army post to get some rest. We were shown that there was one bunk there, and it was indicated that we could share it in shifts. They insisted that I go first as I was the ranking officer—they must have had a book showing the rank of each American soldier. I accepted and tried to sleep. I guess I did, for soon, I was awakened when the interpreter arrived.

There was much commotion and protocol, and formal introductions all around, but the interpreter was not exactly what we had expected; his English was hopeless. In the meantime, George was out there somewhere, and we had to find him. This we explained to the interpreter as well as we could, and to all of those present, and the interpreter spoke to the others for us.

The Rescue Party

Now, things started happening quickly. We were told through the interpreter that they would all help us look for George. The whole village turned out to help find George, it seems! We could see that they were ready to go out and help us in our search, and we all left the village together.

As we approached the outskirts of the area that we planned to search, I suggested that we break up into three groups. I cannot now recall my reasons, but I had Dan take the main road with the village chiefs, while Warren took his group of perhaps 60 villagers up to the left side of the small valley we were in.

Dan stayed on the roadway with the interpreter while I took another group and scattered them out along the right side of the valley, following the ridge of a hill to the south in our search area. Warren took another group off the opposite side of the road and followed the ridge on that side of the valley as we proceeded slowly toward where we concluded George might have landed.

We spread out in a fashion to cover the area better and had been on this effort for about an hour or so. We had not been traveling too long when there was a great commotion on the roadway and we were all waved to come down to the road to where Dan was with his group.

We went immediately. There was much commotion and protocol, for the interpreter had been inquiring of the travelers on the road about seeing anything of our missing airman. There was much excitement as the searchers discovered that, yes, indeed, someone had found George on the roadway the night before and had taken him home with them to spend the night. They would be bringing him to us this day.

What good news, even though we could not yet understand whether George was injured or not. It seemed that he had spent the night with the people who found him and took him into their home, and that they would bring him to us that afternoon in the village. Wow! George have been okay, we thought, since they did not mention anything about injuries that we could determine.

Wonderful news! And now, we all headed back to the village to wait for George to be with us. We returned to the Chinese Army outpost and rested in shifts until later that afternoon when George arrived.

Meanwhile, in the Chinese Army outpost building, a man started boiling water in a wok. He put something that looked like lard on the surface and was about to break an egg on the surface, but I was afraid this would not be too sanitary for us. I explained as best I could that we would like to put the egg into the boiling water and let it get hard inside, instead.

He did not understand, I am sure, but he agreed, and pretty soon we had some hard-boiled eggs to eat. There must have been something else to go with the eggs, but I cannot recall what it was, but my, those boiled eggs tasted mighty good.

George arrived! We listened to his story about the people finding him, taking him home, and bedding him down with them—the Chinese slept all in one bed, toe-to-toe, and they put him into that bed with them. He appeared to be okay until we told him about his parachute being damaged.

He had not realized this happened and quickly inspected his chute. When he saw that there was a piece missing, he looked a little pale, and after that, he was more subdued than before. I'm sure he now realized how close to death he had been.

We asked our interpreter to notify our squadron that we were now all in one group and not injured. I was not sure how long the Army waited before sending a MIA (Missing-in-Action) report to our relatives at home. Now that we were together again, it was only a question of how we would get back to our base, wherever that was.

Riding with the Chinese Army

We were informed that a Chinese Army truck was about to leave for the large city to the north of us, and we could ride on that truck as far as we wished. The truck probably weighed five or six-tons and was loaded with at least eight tons of assorted freight, which was hanging over the side rails. It was their typical charcoal burner-type vehicle, which started on rice alcohol, and after it was underway, the methane gas from the charcoal burner would kick in and the alcohol would be shut off.

On hills, it seemed to me that the alcohol would have to be added again to get us up the hills. We were in a mountainous area, and as I recall, the cab of the truck was only large enough to hold the driver and two of us, so someone had to ride on top of this mess.

It was cold, and the rugs, or a covering of some kind, used to help ward off the wind and cold on the outdoor passengers, didn't help much. I believe we exchanged places at some point so that we each had a turn at riding in the comfort of the drafty truck cab.

My memory says we drove all night and into the next day before we came to a place to spend the night. The sights we saw were beautiful, even in the cloudy, sometimes windy weather. We saw strange-looking mountains, like ice cream cones turned upside down, poking up into the cloudy sky. It was incredibly beautiful country, but due to the weather, it was a dismal ride all the way, in spite of the great scenery. It snowed some more on occasion as well.

I recall that we were on the road about three nights before reaching Kweiyang, which was the "large town to the north," where they were headed. On one of these nights, we stayed with some of our own troops—either OSS or some of the Graves and Records Companies that go in to retrieve deceased crews from the wrecks. But on one of the other nights, we stayed at a Chinese outpost of some size. There were some American soldiers attached to this unit, it seems.

Gombay!

We arrived at one Chinese Army outpost, and after we had located our sleeping quarters and cleaned up, we were invited up to the second or third floor of this large Chinese-style building. This turned out to be a large dining hall with possibly four big round tables, tablecloths on and all.

We were treated like heroes of some sort, although I certainly did not feel anything like a hero after losing a brand-new C-47. But a toast was in order. They toasted us, "Gombay!" This means "bottoms up."

They had placed small ceramic shot glasses in front of us, tiny cups filled with rice whiskey. There were speeches made in Chinese, and someone tried to translate for us in English what had been said. Basically, it was:

"Welcome, and thank you Americans for helping us in this war effort." Then it was more "Gombay," and I don't think that any of us were feeling any pain at that point. And then the food started coming.

In the center of the room on a lazy Susan was a large, round tray with a charcoal fire burning at the center. There were perhaps seven or eight compartments, and we were told that all of these were rice dishes, each prepared in a different manner. They all tasted wonderful. Some had prunes, some oranges, some were sweet, some sour—all were delicious, or at least in my condition.

All through the meal, the Gombay cups were kept filled. Later, I found out that all we had to do was turn our cups over and they would stop filling them up. At any rate, we were treated very graciously and treated to a very delicious banquet. This was a very pleasant and unexpected surprise, given our circumstances and all the things that could have happened.

We continued on our way the next day, rattling along in the coal-burner, and finally arrived at Kweiyang where we spent the night. At Kweiyang, we worked our way back to a place that had a very small hospital, where they checked us out. George, who had been a glider pilot in Burma until he injured his back, had now reinjured his back on this bailout and was in pain.

They checked him out, gave us all a clean bill of health, and sent us on our way. We went to eat and all ate in the Officer's Mess. I was expecting to be told our Enlisted Men would have to eat in the Enlisted Men's Mess, but that never happened. Either they knew why we wanted to eat together, or our being armed indicated we were a combat air crew and perhaps that settled the matter. The subject never came up, so we shall never know why they let us eat in the Officer's Mess.

But we entered Kweiyang with the Chinese Nationalist Army and left Kweiyang on a US Army vehicle—a US weapons carrier. We all sat in the back on the hard wooden seats, bouncing along with the mail and the other freight. It was several more uncomfortable days of travel before we got back to our base at Chungking, but at last we got there.

Seeing Ghosts

When we walked back into base, boy, everyone was surprised to see us! It was like they saw a ghost, and at first, everyone was quiet. After they all said how glad they were glad that we were back, though, I discovered that my air mattress was missing. When I asked where it was, I was told, "Oh, Charley Stratton borrowed it."

So, I went looking for Charley, tracked him down, and retrieved my air mattress. He said he had just borrowed it till I got back, but I wonder if any of them had expected to ever see us again. Probably not, many of our crews did not come back when they went missing.

Several days passed before we were each asked what happened, just for the record. Other than the one meeting that was attended by Rasmussen[6] and Jack Cooney, nothing was ever said to me again about our loss of one C-47. But we were told that over 90 aircraft had been lost in various parts of China that night due to bad weather.

So, we were lucky to have survived, and George later received his luggage that had been on board the Able Queen, so she must have been found and used for salvage parts.

In my original story, I felt that we had landed approximately 150 miles south of Kweiyang. As I look at the map, I am not sure now that it was that far south. However, the roads were unbelievably bad, so the three days on that truck seemed like at least 150 miles. As close as I can read them, the coordinates for Kweiyang are:

106 deg. 40" East Longitude, 26 deg. 35" North Latitude

---

[6] Major James Rasmussen, Commander, 27th Troop Carrier Squadron.

We were lost in an area so remote that they didn't even know the Chinese Flag and could not read their own country's language, as was written on our flags. Only one person in that village had some knowledge of written language, and he was the mayor.

But, we all made it back in once piece and it is a good story because of how it ended, it could have ended a lot differently. Don't forget, there are still over 3,000 MIA left behind in China and Burma. Nobody ever knew what happened to them.

However, the real story here, I feel, is not about soldiers and battles but the real story lives somewhere out there in the "boondocks," where the real people are—no politics, no games, just nice people who go out of their way to help you.

This ends my story of being lost in a remote mountainous area of China, but I will never forget the 15 months I spent inside that scenic country, helping them fight their enemy and trying to keep my crew safe.

Booklet given to US American airmen in China by Army
with Chinese phrases to use in case of bailout.

CHAPTER 13

ALL LANDINGS ARE HAPPY LANDINGS

By May 1945, several pilots and crew members had accumulated more than enough combat hours and/or points to our credit to make us eligible for rotation, and home for a while. The war was far from over, as far as we knew at the time, but we were all in need of rest, or at least a trip home.

My last flight to complete a mission was in early May, and now, the orders would come to send us on our way. Four pilots and nine crew members finally received orders to depart the China Theater of Operations for a visit back to the good ol' USA.

We were flown to Kunming from our base of operations at Chengkung Airfield, just south of Kunming. We reported to the Air Transport Command Operations shack and loaded onto a C-46 transport for the first leg of our trip home. There were five of our squadron on this flight.

The pilots going home were Joe Julliet, Bernard Powers, Eugene Trent, and myself (Bob Binzer). Crew members also on this trip with us were Joe Feola, Ansel Jamison, and I believe seven others, but for some reason, I cannot recall their names at this time.

When it was my turn to leave China, I was eager to head home to the good ol' USA, and in June 1945, twelve of us started on our way home. We were assigned a C-46, like the one we first flew on coming into China. Eager to get home, this was just another ride on a C-46 to me, but with different passengers. But as before, we were not too happy about flying in C-46s with pilots we didn't know because we knew we still faced all the same perils that we had in the beginning.

The weather for our departure was about normal for this time of the year in China, and the aircraft was full, as far as seats available for passengers. Our luggage was in front of us on the floor. Altogether, there were probably anywhere from 45 to 55 passengers on board, anticipating this eventful trip to the United States. Our first stop would be Chabua, in upper Assam, India.

After we loaded, the first problem that I could see was a young man who was really troubled. He probably had some problems to begin with, even before being on this flight. I did not know him; he was not one of our squadron. The troubled man appeared to be having a hard time breathing and was generally uncomfortable. He cried out,

"We won't have to jump out, will we?"

As time to go got closer, he got really upset, still being worried about having to jump out of the plane. One of our other pilots was there too, and we all tried to console him, but none of us could.

It was soon time to take our seats, and we had done all that we could to talk this man down. The noise of the engines made it hard to hear, but the young man was still loud enough that we could all hear him.

Soon, we were climbing into the clouds, and we kept climbing. Climbing on course was a long process due to the field elevation at Kunming and the altitude we needed to reach in order to clear the mountains on our route to India. We had been climbing for quite a while, perhaps two hours; it was dark out, but we were not yet "On Top."

We started to play cards, and everything was quite calm, I thought, until about an hour-and-a-half into the flight. Still in the weather, and still climbing, the right engine started coughing and acting up. We were playing a game of Casino when the right engine of this C-46 started losing power and became very rough, sputtering.

The thing that I recall was that we continued the game of Casino as though nothing was wrong, although we were no longer playing anything. We were only laying the cards down as if we were playing so that we could watch the effort of the crew of that C-46, who were working like mad to get that engine running again.

Finally, the flight crew feathered the engine. Being so close to the cockpit, I stepped up to the doorway and looked in to see what the situation was. The crew was madly doing all the things they could possibly do to get the engine running again. I could smell the alcohol, used to deice the carburetor, and watched the crew attempting to restart the engine.

At this altitude a C-46, and as loaded as we seemed to be, does not hold altitude on a single engine for very long. Those of us that had observed the procedure going on up front decided that it would not hurt anything if we were wearing our parachutes, instead of just sitting on them. Suddenly, the engine quit. Oh boy, another bailout, and on our way home, too!

We were all sweating, and silently, we pilots got up and quietly put on our parachutes. Then, of course, seeing pilots putting on parachutes, the others on board also thought this was a good idea to put on their chutes, too. Now, we had some pretty anxious passengers to share our fears with as the remaining passengers also strapped up.

At this point, the man across the way became very uneasy. Distraught would be a better description. He looked at me and asked again, "We aren't going to bail out, are we?"

In the calmest manner I could muster up, which probably wasn't any too calm, I attempted to tell him that we probably would not have to bail out. Someone over my shoulder agreed, adding, "No, just don't get back there and block the doorway, though."

This quieted him down some. We pilots, and even some of the crew members who had flown with us, realized that we were most likely around snow-covered Mt. Dali, that was well up around 14,000 feet, and if we were much beyond Mt. Dali, we could possibly be over LoLo country, or at least close to it. We knew the LoLos were noted for cannibalism. A fine kettle of fish we'd be in!

Here we were, on our way home. We had turned in our .45 automatic handguns before leaving the base, and our parachute packs were supposedly supplied with bare necessities for survival in the jungle, not the snow-covered mountains, assuming one survived the parachute landing.

This was a very low point for me. So close to getting home, and yet we still had a long way to travel, just to get to India. My thoughts, between prayers, were of a crew that had started home many months ahead of us, but all perished in a crash over somewhere in north Africa, caused by fire on one or more of their engines. I just prayed that the Good Lord would help us get through this mess.

We were still losing altitude at this point, but after what seemed like an hour, the crew finally managed to restart the engine and once more got some altitude back. Thank the Lord! What a relief—we made it!

Eventually, they did get the engines running again, much to our relief, and before long, it was like nothing had happened at all. We all went to sleep, but this scared us pretty badly in the beginning. The rest of the trip home took us across India to Persia (Iran), Egypt, Libya, Casablanca, the Azores, Newfoundland, and finally, good old New York LaGuardia airport.

What a heaven we found when we stepped off the plane! The GOOD OL' USA! The Red Cross ladies were there to greet us with real stateside milk and cookies and donuts! Nothing ever tasted better. Then, we headed for the phones to call home.

There had been a storm in Southern Indiana, and south of Terre Haute there was no phone service, so that was a letdown for me. I knew my family was anxious, but we were home at last, and so thankful you couldn't put it into words. And eventually, I got home. I was so happy to be home on rotation leave.

August 15th: "*THE WAR IS OVER!*"

That meant I did not have to go back to China! We heard about the bombs being dropped, heard awesome descriptions of the bomb and its effects on the radio. This announcement was a surprise, as much of a surprise as Pearl Harbor had been, but this time everyone was wild with excitement and thanksgiving.

We cheered and cried and thought it appropriate for a celebration.

"We'd better get out to the Club before it gets too crowded," Dad said, and we all piled into the car and headed for the Club—only to find that all establishments were ordered to be closed. So, no party at the club for us, but so much joy.

It was 1945. The year started off with me being in the mountains of China and ended with me being at home on a chicken farm south of Terre Haute, Indiana, with my mother, father and younger brothers and sisters, Vaughn, Rollin, and Doralyn. It was the year that I turned 23—and what a full year, let me tell you! I got my first automobile, and more that I can't recall at the moment, but most of all, I got home.

After the war, once I got back, there were several stops that I wanted to make. One was to visit a man who I mentioned earlier, Mr. Kouloff, who had given me a summer job the year I turned 12. He was very good to me and paid me a quarter for my work sweeping up and cleaning around his shoe repair shop.

That quarter was a fortune to a kid back then, and as I worked, we talked about my dreams of flying and he told me about Russia. He was so proud of his citizenship, I knew he'd have the flag out and be proud of me, so I put on my uniform and stopped to see old Mr. Kouloff with all my medals on. He was really happy and thankful, and so surprised that I even remembered him.

When I think back on my time "over there," the people of China—mostly all peasants—were helpful and friendly, and very curious about us, of course. I guess what I need to say at this point that I don't know of any families that I could identify now to go back and search for to thank them for their help.

It would be a fantastic trip to go back down that valley and thank those people that helped us out when we were down and out and helpless. But heaven only knows who, or where they are today. It was so remote where we were that they didn't even know the Chinese flag, nor could they read their own language as it was written on our flags. Only one person in the village that took us in after we bailed out had some knowledge of the written language.

We have heard that the mainlanders do not, as a rule, like to take the American tourists into these very remote areas that I have been into. Kunming maybe, Chungking for sure, but beyond that, it would have to be a real fly-by-the-wire situation. The politicians themselves may have not been into some of these areas too much. So, I can only guess.

But if he could, a fellow could return there once again to reminisce, and show his family where his parachute landed. Perhaps take a gift to the family that let us into their shack to warm ourselves by the fire until we got our heads screwed on right that cold February night. But will the current Chinese government allow us to go into those areas? I don't believe they will, or have in the past.

And so that is that. This is the end of my story of my time in China, as well as I can remember it. It is something that this old pilot will never forget.

After returning home, I was discharged at Camp Atterbury, where we had a little ceremony, and my time as a Hump Pilot in the Army Air Corps was over.

Heading Home. Casablanca, 1945
(L-R): Lt. Robert Binzer, Lt. Bernard Powers,
Lt. Francis Julliet, Lt. Eugene Trent.

CHAPTER 14

FLYING AGAIN – PROJECT DRIBBLE

In September of 1964 1 began flying weekends for Lane Aviation in Columbus, Ohio, for my first job as a commercial pilot. It was good to fly again and be paid for it. I was giving people rides or tours around Columbus and did the occasional charter.

Bob Varner, the VP of Lane Aviation, and who we knew from our Church in Granville, Ohio, asked me if I had a vacation coming up, and if so, would I like to fly one of our airplanes on a contract with North American Aviation (just across the airfield from us). No problem!

The contract was to fly one of our new Cessna 185s on a trip down to Mississippi that would be in the neighborhood of two weeks in duration. We would be flying out of New Orleans Lakefront Airport. I could not believe it; this was the same air port I had been stationed at in 1941 when

I was in the Army. I told him I would have to see if my wife would go along with this idea, which she did.

It was agreed upon, and I would soon meet with the two engineers from North American Aviation (NAA), who would be flying with me. These two would be installing some equipment in the aircraft, and I would help them with the weight and balance. They had our bird, N2057R, in one of the hangers off to the West, where they were installing their equipment, and I met with the two engineers, Dick Harmer and Charley Cummings.

We went over the equipment, and they explained what our mission was about. The contract was with the US Navy for the purpose of testing the radiometer that had been developed at NAA, Columbus, to see if it would be able to detect an atomic bomb detonated underground.

I was to fly the airplane over with this gear installed at 500 feet. The gear comprised an electronic receiver and recording equipment, with a 4-foot parabolic antenna underneath the airplane. I would fly over the area twice a day, one flight at first light, and one just before sundown. Lane aviation was really a sub contractor in this arrangement that I had signed on to.

I inspected the installation and found the battery had been installed too far back in the tail to have a good balance on our weights, so they moved it up closer to the front, and we passed the weight and balance okay. I would have to make a couple of test flights to see if this all worked out okay and that there would be no problems on the trip.

It was 849 miles down to Lakefront Airport in New Orleans, so I would take the airplane down by myself as Charley and Dick Hamer were flying down on Delta because their luggage and other equipment would not fit in our airplane with them.

I departed on the 14th of September for New Orleans, landed at Nashville, TN, for fuel, and then departed for Hattiesburg, MS, where we would be working from at times. I landed in New Orleans and put the bird in the National Guard Hanger at Lakefront, flying 6.8 hours that day. Then, I checked in at the Fontainebleau Hotel and rested up.

Next morning on the 15th, Tuesday, we got the bird out and installed the camera that had been loaned by the Navy. We then took a 50-minute test hop to check things out. The Navy camera did not work for some reason, and we had no time to go back through all the red tape of exchanging it, so we went shopping and found some movie cameras at Sears that would work.

We wired it in and hoped it would do the job. Dick Harmer bought one, and I bought one that we would have as a backup, plus I could be using it for myself until it was needed for replacement of the other camera.

Our first trip to Hattiesburg (HBG) was one hour and one minute in duration. We had to get permission to make a test run over the target area. "Yuletide Control" was the CP, and we were "Dribble 16."

We had trouble making contact, but after landing again to get things straightened out, we made our first run over the site in 26 minutes. We then made another overflight and went back home and had a fine dinner at Kolb's German Restaurant. I wonder if it is still there.

CHAPTER 15

EPILOGUE

Robert Binzer returned home and began to build a civilian life. After the war ended, work was scarce, and housing even more scarce. Like many other returning veterans, he moved to the city to find work and roomed at the YMCA Hotel. But work and housing were only two of his challenges.

As a result of the constant roar of C-47 and L-5 engines in the uninsulated aircraft he piloted, Bob began losing his hearing. His hearing grew worse, and he was forced to wear transistor-radio-sized hearing aids attached by a wired earpiece.

This must have been difficult for a young man in his 20s to be encumbered with in the time before in-ear hearing aids, but he didn't let it get him down. Refusing Veteran's Benefits for service-related deafness, he insisted, "There's nothing wrong with me," and carried on.

While rooming at the YMCA Hotel in Chicago, he met a beautiful young hotel clerk, my mother, Patricia

Ruth Musick, a college student working there for the summer. They fell in love, married, and had one child, me, divorced a few years later, and Bob moved on.

He was restless, and tried his hand at numerous jobs, eventually joining Sargent & Lundy as a field engineer for power plant construction sites, where he worked until retirement.

His job required him to follow power plant construction projects around the country, and at one site, he met the love of his life, Alyce Moore, a beautiful young company nurse. They married and had three children: Jim, Chip, and Cookie, and many grandchildren and great-grandchildren. The family made many moves, and in each new place, Bob took up a different hobby or interest, but flight was never far from his mind.

He attended all squadron reunions and air shows, visited air force buddies, and once built his own light aircraft, with Alyce learning welding to help him build his dream plane. The craft flew once or twice, and then he sold it. When he couldn't fly anymore, he took up sailing, and he and Alyce performed missionary work at home and abroad.

In 1991, Bob and Alyce returned to China with a Flying Tigers tour to retrace his steps. He said they were greeted like heroes everywhere they went. Near the end of his life, he was selected for the Honor Flight to Washington. Bob and Alyce now rest side-by-side in the Veterans Cemetery at Madison, Indiana—his mission complete.

Reflections

Flying without fear requires faith in three things: your pilot, your aircraft, and your God. Trusting your pilot is a legacy I inherited from my father.

Even though my parents divorced, he made sure I knew the thrill of flight. On divorced-dad-visit days he picked me up, ostensibly to go to the park, but really we drove to a local airport, where he rented a small plane from the flying school and taught me how to fly.

Climbing and banking, swooping and soaring, he explained the importance of updrafts and downdrafts and how dial and lever worked. Peppering his lesson with examples from his war days of how this dial or that lever almost cost them, I learned that if you understand your aircraft, there is nothing at all to fear up in flight.

The highlight of each lesson was when Dad turned the controls over to me. I never felt more important than gripping the "Yolk" and steering. Having such confidence placed in me was pretty heady stuff for an almost eight-year-old.

"Look at you, you're flying a plane," he'd brag, then take back over to show me how to land. "Better not mention this to your mom, though. She might not like it." No kidding!

Over the years, I flew frequently for pleasure and work, always boarding the plane with confidence, but as the decades rolled by, things changed. Pilots got younger, planes got older, and then came hijackings and bombings, air traffic control strikes, and the terrorists.

One stormy day in Chicago when boarding a flight, I glanced into the cockpit to see what looked like two high school kids sitting at the controls. When I realized they were our pilots, I lost my nerve. The pilots that I had learned to trust were pilots like my Dad, daredevils who flew primitive planes by the seat of their pants without reliable communications under the worst conditions. These pilots were not *those* pilots.

After World War II ended, many former flyboys took seats in the cockpits of early airlines, adding experience and safety to the fledgling business. For them, commercial flights must have been a cakewalk, and their smooth flying ensured comfortable flights that helped launch the golden age of air travel, but now they were all retired.

Buckling my seat belt that day, I came face-to-face with the realization that my life now rested in the hands of young, less experienced pilots than my dad in a fierce March windstorm. Were they trained for this? I had to find some way to trust these young pilots, or this was going to be a long, nightmarish flight. But then, I thought of about Dad.

How young he was when he got to China. I thought of the countless dangers he faced daily, and how he taught me to love the freedom of the sky. I reminded myself of the three cornerstones of fearless flying and reconnected with the joy of lifting from terra firma. And then, we rumbled down the runway and took off.

Rainy Horvath, December 9, 2020

Rainy Horvath's flying lesson, 1954

CHAPTER 16

AFTERWORD

Looking back at World War II from the perspective of 2020 and reading accounts like this one about the adventures, difficulties, extraordinary efforts, sacrifices, and reflections of participants, we may be inclined to think in multiple ways about the overall event.

On one hand, we appreciate the hard and often dangerous work done by members of a past generation, which allows us to live in the world we enjoy today. We also celebrate the final victory, remember the losses we suffered, and honor those who served. But at the same time, we wonder if it all might repeat again one day. Also, if we were faced with doing it again, can we really say the sacrifices were worthwhile? Let us consider why they were.

The rise of fascism in Europe and of the Japanese Empire in Asia were not sudden, but were unopposed by most Free World leaders, and, once established, those forces no longer could be safely ignored. When the war started (in 1937 for China and in 1939 within Europe), the USA began—well before the Japanese attack on Pearl Harbor—to assist Allies in both regions with war materials production and select trade restrictions.

Money and supplies were offered through the Lend-Lease Program to Great Britain, Russia, and China, and the position of the US Government on tyrannical hostile actions across the world was clearly stated.

The USA was already involved against the forces of fascism and the Japanese imperialists before December 1941, and this was done because to abandon the world's helpless victims was unacceptable—economically and politically, yes, but also morally, and for the sake of safe-guarding the future well-being of the USA.

While it is true that many (perhaps a majority of) citizens opposed entering the war before December 1941, and whatever their thoughts about its value to themselves might have been, when it became clear that war against such aggressors could not be avoided by the USA, they gave their consent and offered their labor, materials, and lives to serve in the cause of protecting the same freedoms, for others as well as themselves, that their forefathers and fore-mothers had struggled and fought to secure and maintain.

In the CBI Theater, problems abounded, relating to command, communications, supply, simple health maintenance, relations with local peoples, and cooperation between Allies, not to mention the great variety of difficult terrains and climates across these very diverse countries. But despite these impediments and US service people's concerns about their families at home, those who served in China, Burma, and India accomplished meaningful achievements that were essential for helping the victimized residents and everyone at home.

Moreover, their caring efforts and sacrifices were not forgotten in the places where they served. As a visitor to several East Asian countries in recent years, I can emphatically attest that our service people from the World War II era are still honored, thanked, and dearly remembered there.

Memoirs, such as the one presented in this volume, help readers to understand what it was like to be called into service for the sake of others in a time of dire crisis.

Veterans of wars are too often silent about their experiences when confronted by people who were "not there"; thus, these memories are treasures that may assist in our understanding of their thoughts and feelings. These accounts further allow us to learn about long-term coping, steeling ourselves to do what we know we must and should, and preparing ourselves in case a similar set of events ever befalls us again.

Perhaps equally, if not more importantly, we can read these memoirs of wartime survivors to ask questions about how to find the most valuable lessons from unwanted events and to seek to prevent humanity's squalls from developing into such unpredictable and terrible storms.

Dr. David T. Fletcher,
November 26, 2020 *(Thanksgiving Day)*

REFERENCE

China Place Names

1943 Spelling	2020 Spelling
Assam	Chabua Military Air Field
Bishan	Bishan *(10 KM from Chungking*
Chanyi	Zhanyi
ChengKung Airfield	WWII Airfield *(near Kunming)*
Chengtu	Cheng Tu
Chihchiang / Chickiang	Zhejiang
Chungking	Chongqing
Hangchung	Hangcheng
Hsian - Hsian Airfield	Xi'an
Kweiyang	Guiyang
Kunming	Kunming
Liangshan	Lianghan Yi Province
Luliang	Lyuliang
Nanchong	Nanchong

Paoshan	Baoshan
Peishiyi /Paishihyi	BaishiyiAirport
Sian	Xian
Suichuan	Sichaun
Szchewan	Szchewan Province
Tien Soan	Tien Shaun
Yunnanyi	Chuxiong
Yurmani	Yurman
Yangtze	Yangtze River

Leader of the Chinese Nationalist Army - Chiang Kai-shek

GLOSSARY

ADF. Automatic Direction Finder. Used since the 1920s, the ADF (Automatic Direction Finder) automatically points in the direction of the Non-Directional Beacon (NDF) broadcast out from the ground station. The radio waves broadcast create an electromagnetic field like a sine wave that are picked up by the aircraft's ADF.

Aileron. A hinged surface in the trailing edge of an airplane wing, used to control lateral balance.

AVG. American Volunteer Group. Volunteer air units organized by the United States government to aid the Nationalist government of China against Japan, dubbed "The Flying Tigers."

Bulkhead. A dividing wall or barrier between compartments in a ship, aircraft, or other vehicle.

CO. Commissioned Officer

HF Radio. High Frequency electromagnetic radio signal used in aviation for air-to-ground communications.

Letdown, Letting Down. The safe descent of an aircraft to the point that landing procedure can begin.

NCO. Non-Commissioned Officer

Revetment. A barricade of earth or sandbags set up to provide protection from blast or to prevent planes from overrunning when landing.

Rudder. A movable surface, mounted on the trailing edge of the vertical stabilizer, which controls the vertical movement of an aircraft.

USO. United Service Organization. A charitable organization formed in 1941 to serve active-duty service members and military families.

Y-Forces. A command of the Chinese National Revolutionary Army that fought with the Allies in Burma and China. They consisted of 175,000 troops in 15 divisions.

BIBLIOGRAPHY

Works Cited

Personal Collection of Rainy Horvath: Letters, emails, recordings, collected stories and photographs of Robert Binzer.

Works Referenced / For More Reading

Dept. of Air Force, Combat Squadrons of the Air Force Word War II. Air Force History Department, 1982.

Frey-Consten, Dr. Carl. *Tales of the Himalayas*. Self-published, 2002.

Jackson, Daniel. *Famine, Sword, and Fire*. Schiffer Military History, 2015.

Kleiner, Sam. *The Flying Tigers*. Penguin Books, 2019.

Montcastle, John, BG. *China Offensive*. US Army Military History, 2003.

Moseley, George. *The Consolidation of the South China Frontier*. Center for Chinese Studies, 1970.

Romanus, Charles; Sunderland, Riley. *Time Runs Out in the CBI: China Burma India*. US Army Center for Military History, 1999.

Rose, Alexander. *Empires of the Sky.* Random House, New York, 2020.

The Mister. Coleman Flying School Class of 1943 Yearbook. News Syndicate Co., Ltd., 1943.

REFERENCES

Air Transport Command, Jobe, Larry; London, Pradit. "Making of The Hump Documentary Honoring CBI Pilots."

Boomerang Publishers and Video. "Air Transport Command 1943." ATC Association, 1943.

Kaiman, Johnathan. "The Legend of the Blond, Blue-eyed Slave: Retracing a crashed World War II pilot's journey through China." *LA Times*, August 2017.

Johnson, Benjamin A. "From Burma to Berlin: The Development of U.S. Air Transport 1938-1949."

Periscope Film, LLC. "China Crisis: 14th Airforce in China." Army Special Forces Film Project, 1944

Sears, David. "The Hump: Death and Salvation on the Aluminum Trail" *World War II Magazine*, Nov/ Dec 2016.

The Hump Association. "A Fact Sheet for the Hump Operations during WWII." 2010.

Thomas, Nedda R. Hump Pilot: Defying Death Flying the Himalayas During World War II. Aviation History.

Thompson, Ben. "China-Burma-India Theater of World War II." 2000.

US Army Air Force. Pointee-Talkee Book. Carl Warren Weidenburner, 2004, 2015.

White-Theodore, "The Hump: Historic Highway to China was Created by US Heroes." *Life Magazine*, 11 September 1944. Reprinted on History.Net

Weidenburner, Carl Warren, "China-Burma-India: Remembering the Forgotten Theater of World War II." 2003.

PERMISSIONS/
ACKNOWLEDGEMENTS

Grateful thanks to the following corporations and organizations for generously sharing knowledge and permissions for use here.

Carl Warren Weidenburner, "Remembering the Forgotten Theater of War: China-Burma-India.

General Mills Corporate Archivist

Post Consumer Brands Research Group.

PHOTO CREDITS

Personal Photo Collection of Rainy Horvath.

US Army Center for Military History Map Collection (Public Domain).

National Archives Photo Collection (Public Domain).

Carl Warren Weidenburner, CBI-Theater History Collection.

PRIOR PUBLICATION CREDITS

Shortened versions and summaries of some episodes in this memoir previously appeared in the following publications:

Lt. Eugene Trent (RET), 27th Troop Carrier Squad- China-Burma-India 1944-1945, compiled 1996.

Brewer, Howton, Theis. *The China Airlift: Volume III*. China-Burma-India Hump Pilots Association. Turner Publishing, 1991.

Jackson, Daniel. *Famine, Sword, Fire*. Schiffer Military Publishing, 2015.

The Madison Courier. "Flying Tiger." 2013 Airforce Magazine. Date Unknown.

Indiana Historical Society Newsletter, "How Well I Remember." Indiana Historical Society, Date Unknown.

THE END

AUTHOR BIO

 Rainy Horvath wrote award-winning documentation for Fortune 500 companies and taught writing at New York City area colleges, including Fashion Institute of Technology and Marymount College at Tarrytown (now Fordham University). She holds an MFA in creative writing from Manhattanville College, and her short fiction and poetry have been published both online and in print. Rainy lives with her husband in the Hudson River Valley and these days can be found in her garden working on her next novel. The Able Queen is her first book.

Made in United States
Orlando, FL
11 July 2023